Voting Rights in America

The Leadership Conference Education Fund (LCEF) is a non-profit, tax-exempt organization that conducts research and educational activities on civil rights issues. Our goal is to strengthen the nation's commitment to civil rights and equality of opportunity for all. Our work combines a *review* of the progress made in civil rights over the last 40 years, a *focus* on present civil rights abuses, and a *vision* for addressing remaining civil rights challenges. The Leadership Conference Education Fund enjoys a close relationship with the Leadership Conference on Civil Rights, the oldest, largest, and most broadly based civil rights coalition in the country seeking to achieve equality in a free, plural, democratic society. The Leadership Conference on Civil Rights has been at the core of federal civil rights initiatives over the last 40 years.

The Joint Center for Political and Economic Studies is a nonpartisan, nonprofit research institution that uses research and information dissemination to accomplish three objectives: to improve the socio-economic status of black Americans; to increase their influence in the political and public policy arenas; and to facilitate the building of coalitions across racial lines. The Joint Center contributes to the national interest by helping black Americans to participate fully in the political and economic life of our society.

★ VOTING ★ RIGHTS IN AMERICA

Continuing the Quest for Full Participation

INCLUDING AN ESSAY BY BILL CLINTON

MARY FRANCES BERRY ★ DAMON KEITH
ARMAND DERFNER ★ CHARLES V. HAMILTON
KAREN McGILL ARRINGTON
LANI GUINIER ★ JEANETTE WOLFLEY
MARGERET EDDS ★ AL RABY
HENRY DER ★ CELINDA LAKE
DAVID KUSNET

Edited by Karen McGill Arrington
& William L. Taylor

Leadership Conference Education Fund
Joint Center for Political and Economic Studies
Washington, D.C.

Excerpt from *And We Are Not Saved: The Elusive Quest for Racial Justice,* by Derrick Bell, used by permission of Basic Books, Inc., a division of HarperCollins Publishers.

Leadership Conference Education Fund
2027 Massachusetts Avenue, N.W.
Washington, D.C. 20036

Joint Center for Political and Economic Studies
1090 Vermont Avenue, N.W., Suite 1100
Washington, D.C. 20005–4961

Library of Congress Cataloging-in-Publication Data

Voting rights in America : continuing the quest for full participation / edited by Karen McGill Arrington and William L. Taylor.
p.   cm.
Includes papers presented at LCEF's conference in 1988.
Includes bibliographical references.
1. Afro-Americans—Suffrage—History—Congresses.
2. Minorities—Suffrage—United States—History—Congresses.
3. Voter registration—United States—History—Congresses.
I. Arrington, Karen McGill.   II. Taylor, William L.
III. Leadership Conference Education fund.
KF4893.A75V67   1993
324.6'2'0973—dc20   92–37503 CIP

ISBN 0–941410–52–8 (cloth : alk. paper)
ISBN 0–941410–55–2 (pbk. : alk. paper)

Dedicated to the memory of Al Raby and Willie Velasquez, whose contributions to the struggle for voting rights were beyond measure. They will be sorely missed.

Contents

The Impact of the Vote

Citizen Action in Voting

Foreword

The Leadership Conference Education Fund (LCEF) is a nonprofit, tax-exempt research and education organization dedicated to strengthening the nation's commitment to civil rights and equality of opportunity. Pursuant to that goal, LCEF seeks to assess the progress that has been made, analyze ongoing civil rights policies, problems and programs, and determine what steps need to be taken to surmount the barriers that remain to the enjoyment of full civil rights by all our citizens.

In the course of the nation's observance of the bicentennial of the Constitution, LCEF held a conference, called *"200 Years of Expanding the Franchise: Celebrating the Bicentennial of the Constitution,"* to pay tribute to the Founding Fathers for creating a document that allows for its own expansion, and to pay tribute also to the many Americans who have labored for that expansion. The official bicentennial observance extended from 1987 to 1991 in order to include the bicentennial of the ratification of the Bill of Rights. For without the Bill of Rights there would have been much less cause for celebration.

The Constitution is presumably the only document conceived in perfection and dedicated to improvement: "We the people of the United States in order to form a *more perfect* union." The reality, of course, is that the Constitution is not a perfect document and we are not yet a perfect union let alone a *more perfect* one.

Those self-evident truths proclaimed in 1776, that all men are created equal and endowed by their creator with certain inalienable rights, were not so self-evident in 1787, and the stirring three opening words of the Constitution—*We the people*—were not intended and never did apply to every citizen.

But whatever the limitations and imperfections in the Constitution, the genius of the Framers was in making allowances for its expansion and self-correction. They understood that what they were forging was not an immutable document carved in stone but a living Constitution.

ix

The papers contained in this volume, which were presented at LCEF's conference in 1988, trace that process of amendment and expansion by focusing on the franchise, which has been called the crown jewel of American liberty.

The papers examine the treatment of the franchise by the Founding Fathers, review the efforts over the past 200 years to extend the franchise to those to whom it was denied in the Constitution, assess the impact of the vote on the lives of newly enfranchised groups, explore the obstacles that still prevent or make it very difficult for citizens to vote, and examine what further steps might be taken to ensure that the right to vote is enjoyed by each and every American. The struggle to achieve that goal goes back to the earliest days of the Republic; it has been a long, bitter, and, too often, bloody struggle. Many of the authors continue to play a significant role in advancing the goal of equal voting rights for all.

On behalf of LCEF I want to thank a number of people who contributed to the success of the conference and the production of this volume. First, the staff of LCEF: Ralph G. Neas, executive director, who provided overall supervision; Karen McGill Arrington, deputy director, who more than any other individual is responsible for bringing these projects to fruition, and is one of the two editors of the volume and author of the introductory paper; Lisa Haywood, office manager; Fatima McClearn, secretary; and Mary Delaney, office clerk. Thanks also goes to Natalie Shear, who served as coordinator for the conference.

LCEF is also extremely appreciative of the services of William L. Taylor, vice-president of LCEF, the other editor of the volume and author of the Afterword. Bill was a consultant to the conference and served as an overall advisor on this project, as he does on many LCEF projects. His assistance is invaluable.

I would also like to thank Eddie N. Williams, president of the Joint Center for Political and Economic Studies, and Milton Morris, the Center's vice president for Research, as well as the Center's editorial and production staff—Nancy Stella, Marc DeFrancis,

Tyra Wright, and Allison King. Their expertise helped make possible the publication of this project. A very special thanks to Laura Akgulian for her editorial and documentation assistance in preparing this book for print.

Thanks also to the authors for their participation in the conference, for their preparation of the papers for publication, and for their continuing fight to make political participation a reality.

Finally, LCEF would like to express its appreciation to the Ford Foundation for its financial support of the "Expanding the Franchise" conference and the publication of these papers.

LCEF is proud to dedicate this book to the memory of two champions of the struggle to expand the franchise.

Al Raby was chairman of the board of directors of Project Vote! during the last three years of his life. Project Vote!'s primary goal is the registration of minorities and the poor so they will participate in the election process. A civil rights activist in the 1960s, he was Peace Corps director in Ghana during the Carter administration. Al was the late Chicago mayor Harold Washington's 1983 campaign manager and served as the director of the Chicago Commission on Human Relations under Mayor Washington.

Willie Velasquez spent much of his career organizing and then directing the Southwest Voter Registration Education Project (SWVREP) in San Antonio. Willie served as director of SWVREP from its founding in 1974 until his death in 1988. During his tenure, SWVREP undertook more than 960 voter registration campaigns throughout 132 cities and Indian reservations in the six Southwestern states, and successfully prosecuted 82 cases protecting the civil rights of minorities in the Southwest.

The contributions Al Raby and Willie Velasquez made to the struggle for voting rights were beyond measure. They will be sorely missed.

Arnold Aronson
President
Leadership Conference Education Fund

Preface

The Declaration of Independence proclaims that "all men are created equal." But it was not until the ratification of the Fifteenth Amendment, in 1870, that black men in America were granted the right to vote—regardless of "race, color, or previous condition of servitude." And it was another 50 years before black women were enfranchised.

Since its founding in 1970, the Joint Center for Political and Economic Studies has examined black Americans' role in the electorate. In reviewing black voter turnout and registration in both presidential and congressional elections, we have looked at the geographic, political, and economic forces at work. Our findings have been enlightening as well as confounding.

As blacks have become more conscious of policy issues that affect their well-being, their level of political activism has grown. Both strong voter mobilization appeals and court challenges to discriminatory electoral practices have contributed to the rise in black voter participation. Key legislative efforts have played a vital role as well. The U.S. Constitution, in its original form, was never enough to guarantee *all* citizens a voice in our democracy.

Black voter participation has grown tremendously since the passage of the Voting Rights Act of 1965. The evidence is in the numbers: prior to 1965, only 7 percent of eligible blacks were registered to vote in Mississippi; in 1990, 71.4 percent were registered, according to the U.S. Census Bureau. In 1970, there were 1,200 black elected officials; at the end of 1991, there were 7,500.

Key political victories—for example, the elections of Virginia Governor L. Douglas Wilder, Mississippi Congressman Mike Espy, and New York Mayor David Dinkins—all hinged on high black voter turnout (as well as strong support from white voters). Rev. Jesse Jackson's impressive 1984 and 1988 presidential bids can be directly attributed to a strong black turnout at the polls.

With the completion of the recent congressional redistricting process, 13 new black congresspersons were expected to be elected in November 1992, to join the current 26 members of the Congressional Black Caucus. At the same time, more than 100 new black state legislators were expected to be elected, expanding the total of such legislators to 560.

Yet, despite these gains, much of the road toward equal representation remains ahead of us. Even with a House of Representatives comprised of nearly 10 percent black members, blacks would still be underrepresented, since they make up 13 percent of the population. And, of course, there are no black members of the U.S. Senate. (At this writing, black Democrat Carol Moseley Braun is favored to win a Senate seat from Illinois.)

The Voting Rights Act has significantly reduced barriers to black political participation, and it continues to be a major bulwark against attempts to dilute the black vote. Clearly, it is still urgently needed.

What is also needed is the continued efforts on the part of black leaders and organizations to stress the importance of political participation and to use their energy and resources in a nonpartisan way to increase the levels of registration and turnout. One such organization that continues to provide leadership in this area is the National Coalition on Black Voter Participation. This unique coalition comprises 88 black organizations and labor unions, and both the Republican and Democratic parties. Now in its 16th year, the National Coalition is the only full-time voter mobilization enterprise in the African American community.

The Joint Center is proud to be a co-publisher of this volume of essays which underscores the importance of voting rights and urges eternal vigilance in protecting them. The goal of *Voting Rights in America* is to make readers aware of the importance of enfranchisement and enlighten them as to the struggles and accomplishments of those who fought, and continue to fight, for this right. Only when there are no remaining barriers to voting will we truly have a nation of liberty and justice for all.

Eddie N. Williams
President
Joint Center for Political and
Economic Studies

Introduction

David Kusnet

During the final years of the 1980s and into the 1990s, Americans watched with fascination while peoples throughout the world took to the streets to demand democracy. Sometimes we witnessed horrifying violence, as when protesters were mowed down in China's Tiananmen Square and the Rumanian city of Timisoara.

We saw peaceful mass protests, as when "people power" marchers in Manila demanded that Ferdinand Marcos acknowledge defeat in the presidential election, when the Polish Solidarity movement and the Czechoslovak Civic Forum ousted Communist regimes, and when black South Africans welcomed Nelson Mandela after his release from prison into a society in which he still could not vote. And, in August 1991, Boris Yeltsin stood on top of a tank and inspired an aroused citizenry to resist the military coup that would have restored Communist dictatorship.

But, often, what inspired American audiences was a simpler spectacle, replayed in nation after nation. In the Philippines, Chile, Poland, Czechoslovakia, Brazil, East Germany, and Hungary, people flocked to the polls for what were often the first free elections in their lifetimes. The sight was a reassuring image for Americans because it corresponded to our most fundamental concept of what democracy means.

Americans, after all, are the heirs to a revolution spurred by the slogan "no taxation without representation." Our Declaration of

1

Independence proclaimed that governments derive "their just powers from the consent of the governed." And our most beloved President explained that our Civil War was fought to ensure the survival of "government of the people, by the people, and for the people." Implicit in all these statements of the American creed is one fundamental idea: the franchise is central to democracy.

If democracy is America's civil religion, voting is its most important sacrament. Thus, election coverage often presents not only the smiling or sorrowful winners and losers but also the scenes at our polling places: young and old, women and men, black and brown and white, some in business suits and some in blue jeans, all equal participants in the drama of democracy. That image gives meaning to the first three words of the United States Constitution, "We the people."

But, as Barbara Jordan reminded the nation in the midst of its bicentennial celebration, when the Constitution's Framers wrote the words "We the people," the system they created enfranchised only some of the people. They did not recognize the right to vote for black people and women. In most states, the franchise was reserved for white, propertied men, and in many states Catholics, Jews, and other groups were specifically disenfranchised.

Over the ensuing two centuries, the growth of American democracy can be gauged by the expansion of the eligible electorate, with state and federal laws, constitutional amendments, and Supreme Court decisions recognizing the voting rights of the unpropertied, religious minorities, African Americans, women, Native Americans, Hispanics and other language minorities, 18-year-olds, and others who had been shut out of the political process. Indeed, the expansion of the franchise is so central a theme in our history that half of the 16 constitutional amendments adopted after the Bill of Rights have addressed voting.

While the growth of our democracy can be measured by the inclusion of these potential voters, the problems of our democracy are underscored by the disturbingly low participation rate among

2

the eligible electorate. During the 1980s, little more than half of all eligible voters cast ballots in presidential elections and just over a third voted in state and local elections. Fewer still participated in other aspects of the political process, whether it was party caucuses and primaries, civic activism, or public debate on local, state, national, and international issues. If, as Alexis de Tocqueville wrote in 1833, politics is "the only pleasure an American knows," then, for a growing percentage of our people, that pleasure is at best a vicarious one.

Of the millions of Americans who sit out the democratic process, some have been shut out by barriers that are the vestiges of the crudest forms of exclusion and intimidation of the past. Others are discouraged by the uniquely American system of voter registration that places the burden on the individual voters, rather than the government, to make sure that their names are on the roll of eligible voters. A growing number of other Americans apparently have been turned off by a political system increasingly characterized by negative campaigning, by reliance upon the mass media rather than grassroots organization, and by the excessive influence of wealthy contributors. Still others seem to have tuned out entirely on public events, from their local school boards, their city halls and state houses, to Capitol Hill and the White House.

The exclusions that marred American democracy at its founding, the historic struggles against disenfranchisement, the current efforts to remove the remaining barriers to political participation and to mobilize those who are shut out, tuned out, or turned off—all are discussed in this book on political participation in America, from the era of the Framers to the onset of the Twenty-first century.

It is based on the papers and presentations at a conference held in May 1988 by the Leadership Conference Education Fund and made possible by a grant from the Ford Foundation. These papers are a reminder that there is more to the drama of American democracy than those photographs of a cross-section of citizens, waiting their turn to vote on election day.

The authors present other images as well, snapshots of the struggle to extend the most basic right in our democracy—images of ordinary citizens participating in politics or pursuing, often at great peril, the right to participate that was previously denied them. Triumph and tragedy, peaceful protest and state violence, and the inspiring spectacle of people winning a voice in their own destiny—all this has happened within recent memory in our own country, just as in Eastern Europe and East Asia, South Africa and South America.

These papers, by activists and scholars and by many who have earned both titles, provide both historical and contemporary perspectives on the struggle to expand political participation in the United States. To read these papers is to be compelled to consider three theses about American democracy:

- First, the American political system was founded on a creative contradiction: its expansive claims of democracy clashed with the social, economic, and political realities that excluded much of the population from the rights of self-government.
- Second, largely through the struggles of the disenfranchised, American democracy has grown as the electorate has grown, and, today, our society comes closer than before to keeping the promises of the Declaration of Independence, the Constitution, the Bill of Rights, the Civil War Amendments, and other fundamental documents of our system of government.
- Third, the American system still falls far short of the goal of full political participation by all its citizens. Still remaining are barriers to political empowerment which can be eliminated, now as in the past, through movements that mobilize people to fight for their rights.

An honest reading of American history can honor the Framers for beginning history's most successful experiment in democracy while also acknowledging that the men who devised the American system were products of their time, place, and position, and, therefore, profoundly ambivalent about popular self-government. This ambivalence was reflected not only in the failure to expand the franchise beyond white men of property but also in the creation of a system that originally provided for the indirect election not only of the President but the Senate.

As Justice Thurgood Marshall observed in a much-quoted speech in 1987, the Constitution was "defective from the start" since it failed to recognize the rights of blacks and women. In his paper, Judge Damon Keith discusses the compromises that emerged at the Constitutional Convention and set the course for the country until the Civil War. Delegates from the Northern states "conceded the existence of slavery to the South in order to make the South a party to the union" in return for an agreement that "the importation of slaves would cease in the year 1808." While, as Judge Keith notes, the delegates did not consider enfranchising the slaves, they did debate at great length whether the slaves should be counted while apportioning congressional seats and assessing federal taxes. As Judge Keith explains: "This question was resolved by the pernicious 'three-fifths rule,' which required that the vote be in proportion to the whole number of white and other free citizens and three-fifths of 'all other persons' except Indians not paying taxes. The 'all other persons' were, of course, slaves."

While America's original sin—the toleration of slavery and disenfranchisement—was spelled out in the original language of Article I, Section 2, there also were other barriers to voter participation at the state and national levels. The Constitution gave states the rights to set the qualifications for voting, and they variously denied the vote to blacks, women, Catholics, Jews, Indians, servants, and, quite frequently, anyone who didn't own property.

Over the two centuries since the ratification of the Constitution, the nation's political history has been "the history of barriers [to voting] erected and barriers erased," as Mary Frances Berry observes.

When the "gentry politics" of the Framers was replaced by the "common man politics" of Andrew Jackson, the states reduced or eliminated property requirements for voting. Voter participation rose from 27 percent of the eligible electorate in 1824, when the aristocrat John Quincy Adams defeated Jackson for the presidency; to 58 percent in 1828, when Jackson defeated Adams; to 80 percent in 1840, when the hero of the battle of Tippecanoe, William Henry Harrison, was elected in a rollicking campaign featuring torchlight parades, coonskin caps, and the slogan "Tippecanoe and Tyler, too."

But, as Karen McGill Arrington notes, while voter participation was expanding among white men, eight Northern and border states were disfranchising blacks. By 1838, the constitutions of Connecticut, Delaware, Kentucky, Maryland, New York, North Carolina, Tennessee, and Virginia had been amended to exclude blacks—even free men—from voting. By the time of the Civil War, the only states allowing free blacks to vote were New Hampshire, Vermont, Rhode Island, and Massachusetts.

It took the nation's bloodiest war, the Civil War, to enact what historian Charles Hamilton calls "the Second Constitution"—the Thirteenth, Fourteenth, and Fifteenth amendments, which "promised something the Framers denied." The Thirteenth Amendment formally abolished slavery throughout the United States; the Fourteenth Amendment recognized the concept of national citizenship, forbidding the states to abridge the rights of their citizens; and the Fifteenth Amendment declared simply that "The right of citizens of the United States to vote shall not be denied or abridged by the United States or by any State on account of race, color, or previous condition of servitude."

Tragically, the promise of the post-Civil War amendments— that the power of the federal government would incorporate every state into a system of national citizenship—was broken after the disputed election of 1876, when the Republicans retained the Presidency in return for an agreement with Southern Democrats to withdraw federal troops from the former Confederate states. With Reconstruction halted, the South made every effort to undo the enfranchisement and even the emancipation of black people. Between 1890 and 1910, 12 states enacted laws that did not mention race but were widely used to prevent non-whites from voting—poll taxes, literacy tests, and other barriers—while "grandfather clauses" protected the rights of whites whose grandfathers had been enfranchised.

Meanwhile, as Frances Fox Piven and Richard A. Cloward discuss in *Why Americans Don't Vote*, new barriers were erected throughout the nation to restrict the political power of low-income people, white as well as black. Alarmed by the growing strength of immigrants and industrial workers, particularly in the big cities, wealthy "reformers" instituted restrictive voter registration systems. Similarly, in the South, poll taxes and literacy tests were increasingly used to disenfranchise not only blacks but poor whites as well. Thus, between 1888 and 1924, voter participation fell from 64 percent to 19 percent of the eligible electorate in the South, from 86 percent to 55 percent in the North and West, and from 81 percent to 49 percent nationally.[1] But in Berry's continuing cycle of "barriers erected and barriers erased," by the second decade of the Twentieth century, the expansion of the electorate and of democracy resumed once again.

The movement begun in the 1840s to enfranchise women, as Dr. Berry notes, included "civil disobedience, picketing, marching, jailing, and the acts of courageous people including Carrie Chapman Catt, Alice Paul, Ida Wells Barnett and Mary Church Terrell." The women's suffrage movement culminated with the ratification of the 19th Amendment in 1920.

It was 100 years after the passage of the Civil War amendments that their promise of enfranchisement for black people in the South was fulfilled. As Dr. Berry notes, the struggle for voting rights was part of the struggle for racial equality which included the founding of the National Association for the Advancement of Colored People

7

(1909), the Supreme Court decision outlawing grandfather clauses (1915), the creation of the Fair Employment Practices Commission (1941), the first civil rights plank in a Democratic National Platform (1948), the desegregation of the armed forces (1948), the Supreme Court decision outlawing public school segregation (*Brown*, 1954), the Montgomery Bus Boycott (1955), the freedom rides and sit-ins of the 1950s and '60s, the Civil Rights Acts of 1957 and 1964, the March on Washington of 1963, and the Mississippi Freedom Summer (1964), to name just a few historic milestones.

Even after desegregation had begun in public schools and public accommodations, most black people in the South were still disenfranchised by various legal devices and by outright physical intimidation. When the Voting Rights Act became law in 1965, only 31 percent of all black people of voting age were registered to vote in the seven states covered by the new law: Virginia, North Carolina, South Carolina, Georgia, Alabama, Mississippi, and Louisiana. In Mississippi, where "Freedom Summer" volunteers had organized for voting rights the year before (and where Medgar Evers, Jimmie Lee Jackson, James Chaney, Andrew Goodman, and Michael Schwerner had been murdered), only seven percent of voting-aged blacks were allowed to register.

Throughout the Deep South, as civil rights attorney Armand Derfner recalls in his paper, the local authorities displayed seemingly limitless energy and ingenuity in their efforts to disenfranchise black men and women:

> And some of the tactics, of course, were spectacular. It was not just the specific barriers—literacy tests, poll taxes, and so on—but the fact that the right to vote was in the hands of local princes and dukes known as registrars and clerks that gave them just all the freedom in the world. Each time one tactic was eliminated, another one would replace it until Congress could be stirred to act, and that was inevitably a losing race for black voters.

8

These injustices were brought before a worldwide audience early in 1965 when Martin Luther King led nonviolent protests in Selma, Alabama, the seat of a county whose population was 57.6 percent black but where only 2.1 percent of the registered voters were black. (In Selma itself, only 156 of more than 15,000 blacks of voting age were registered to vote.) As that saying from the 1960s would have it, the whole world was watching on Sunday, March 7, 1965, when horseback-riding state police tear-gassed and clubbed a crowd of civil rights marchers who had gathered at the foot of the Edmund Pettus Bridge, just outside of Selma.

As attorney Derfner writes:

> The dramatic culmination of these developments was the Voting Rights Act of 1965, which represented a radical shift away from the earlier approaches. Specifically, the heart of the Act was the banning of literacy tests, as well as the virtual banning of poll taxes. The key to the Act, though, was not so much the specifics as the fact that control over the process was taken out of the arbitrary hands of the local clerks and registrars, and the reality of this change was brought home to them by sending federal examiners to register voters themselves in the most never-say-die counties. The shift in power was further brought home by the preclearance provision of Section 5, which told the counties that they could no longer stay one step ahead of the law but would have to get permission to change their laws, and that permission would come not from hometown courts, but from Washington, D.C.

The Voting Rights Act, as Derfner notes, was "strong medicine"—so strong that it was drafted as temporary legislation, due to expire in five years.

It has been a tribute to the importance Americans place upon the right to vote—and to the strength and sophistication of the civil rights coalition—that the Voting Rights Act has not only been

9

renewed but also strengthened each time that it came before Congress. In 1970, despite political maneuvering by the Nixon Administration, the Voting Rights Act was renewed, and it outlawed literacy tests throughout the nation. In addition to the seven states originally affected by the law, tests were suspended in 20 more states, including California, New York, and Illinois. The 1970 extension also helped language-minority voters by providing for assistance for voters for whom English is not their first language.

The Voting Rights Act was extended again in 1975, this time with new protections requiring bilingual ballots in communities with large language-minority populations. Arizona, Texas, and parts of California and Florida—all areas with large numbers of Hispanics and, in California, Asian Americans as well—were now protected under provisions of the Voting Rights Act requiring federal approval for revisions in state and local election laws and procedures.

In the years following the passage of the Act, the same ingenuity that had created literacy tests, poll taxes, and other barriers to voter registration was now applied to make sure that even if black people (or Hispanics or Asian Americans) could cast their votes, they wouldn't count as much as other people's. Electing city council or county board members at-large, rather than from districts; annexing predominantly white areas onto predominantly black districts; gerrymandering districts to minimize the number with predominantly black electorates; annexing predominantly white suburbs onto predominantly black cities and towns; and manipulating the number, locations, and hours of voter registration and polling sites—all these tactics came to be used to dilute black, Hispanic, and Asian-American voting power.

As the 1980s began, new challenges emerged to voting rights and political empowerment for people who had only recently been enfranchised. In the spring of 1980, the U.S. Supreme Court ruled that election laws—in this case, an at-large system in Mobile, Alabama—could not be challenged on the grounds of its racially discriminatory impact unless it could also be established that there was discriminatory intent in adopting such procedures. A year later, the Reagan Administration took office, and, as Derfner recalls, civil rights advocates were anxious that the new president "planned to turn the clock back, and ... brought into office a gang of people who were deadly serious about it."

Thus, there was a special sense of urgency to the effort to renew the Voting Rights Act in 1982, a story told by Lani Guinier, assistant counsel of the NAACP Legal Defense Fund. When the civil rights coalition began planning strategy a year before the law came up for renewal, potential obstacles loomed. A Republican Senate had been elected in the Reagan landslide of 1980, and, instead of Edward Kennedy, the Senate Judiciary Committee was now chaired by Strom Thurmond, who had left the Democratic Party in 1948 in protest against its strong civil rights platform plank. Moreover, the Senate Subcommittee on the Constitution, which had jurisdiction over voting rights, was now chaired by Orrin Hatch, who had recently opposed strengthening the Fair Housing Act. Facing such seemingly unfavorable circumstances, the civil rights groups might have been strongly tempted simply to support the renewal of the existing Voting Rights Act, rather than push for enactment of an even stronger law.

But, as Guinier recalls:

> The civil rights groups met in 1981 and with a lot of guts—perhaps a lot more guts than brains at the time—decided that we were going to go for broke: not only were we going to extend the Voting Rights Act temporary provisions that had first been enacted in 1965 and were due to expire in August 1982. But we were going to overturn the Supreme Court decision in *City of Mobile* v. *Bolden* requiring proof of discriminatory purpose in the adoption or maintenance of an election system. We were going to re-establish a results test in the Voting Rights Act. And, if that weren't enough, we were going

11

to join with our Latino allies and extend the bilingual assistance provision.

Hearings on the legislation proved persuasive to many members of Congress from both parties and across the political spectrum. Witnesses told many troubling but true stories of official attempts to undermine or eliminate the right to vote.

Passing the House by an overwhelming 389 to 24 margin, the Senate by 85 to 8, and signed by President Reagan on June 18, 1982, the Voting Rights Act was extended for 25 years—well into the next century. But, as one conference participant after another made clear, there are no lasting victories in the effort to expand voting in America.

Journalist Margaret Edds told the conference about her journey in 1985 to the seven states originally covered by the Voting Rights Act—Virginia, North Carolina, South Carolina, Georgia, Alabama, Mississippi, and Louisiana. Here she found that the struggles to enact the law and fulfill its promise had achieved remarkable gains. In 1985, there were more than 2,300 black elected officials in these seven states, compared to scarcely 300 black elected officials in the entire nation in 1965. Twenty years after the passage of the Voting Rights Act, black mayors presided in Atlanta, New Orleans, Birmingham, and dozens of small cities. Douglas Wilder, who would in 1989 become the first black governor in the nation since Reconstruction, had in 1985 been elected lieutenant governor of Virginia.

Edds also noted that in the seven Voting Rights Act states, where 31 percent of voting-age blacks had been registered in 1965, that figure had grown in 20 years to 66 percent. Mississippi, last in the nation in 1965 with only seven percent black voter registration, now led the nation with 86 percent black registration. In Louisiana, Mississippi, and South Carolina, higher percentages of blacks than of whites were registered to vote.

By the mid-1980s, as Karen McGill Arrington notes, more than half of the nation's 6,400 black elected officials came from communities that had been covered by provisions of the Voting Rights Act. Part of the explanation is that these communities have large black electorates; part of the explanation may also be that the struggle against discriminatory electoral practices helped activate and motivate black voters in these communities.

On the other side of the ledger, Edds and other conference participants found continuing barriers to black political empowerment—and limits to the impact of political change upon social and economic structures. In the seven Voting Rights Act states, while blacks were 26 percent of the population, they held only 8-10 percent of elective offices. As Edds observes, political change did not automatically produce social and economic change:

> In numbers of elected officials, ease of registration, disappearance of violence, and integration of work places and public facilities, the South of 1985—and 1988—would have been unrecognizable in 1965. Yet, for many, in terms of schools, residential housing, and social patterns, life is almost as segregated today as 20 years ago.

But this may not be the end of the story. The very conditions that reflect the limits of political action—the persistence of poor housing, inadequate schools, and economic inequality—may motivate more voters to participate in politics in an effort to elect public officials who will take action against these problems.

As several papers in this book explain, the struggles of black Americans inspired other groups victimized by discrimination to confront the obstacles to their own political participation.

The women's suffrage movement included many abolitionists, and after the Fifteenth Amendment enfranchised black men, these activists campaigned for the enfranchisement of women, a goal that was attained nationally in 1920 with the passage of the Nineteenth Amendment. But, as Celinda Lake reports, voter participation among women increased gradually at first during the 1920s and

13

expanded rapidly only as recently as the 1960s and '70s—coinciding with the rise of the women's movement and the growth in the number of women who work outside the home. Today, women are a majority of the actual, as well as the potential, electorate.

Political participation among Hispanics also increased dramatically during the 1970s and '80s. With the passage of the Voting Rights Amendments of 1975, Congress found that Hispanics and other language minorities faced two kinds of barriers to full political participation. As the U.S. Civil Rights Commission noted in a 1981 report on voting rights:

> ... because of the denial of equal educational opportunities by state and local governments, language minorities experienced severe disabilities and illiteracy in the English language that, together with English-only elections, excluded them from participation in the electoral process. Congress, therefore, determined that to enforce the Fourteenth and Fifteenth Amendments to the U.S. Constitution, it was necessary to eliminate such discrimination by prohibiting English-only elections and by prescribing other remedial devices.

In the 1975 Voting Rights Amendments, Congress required that, in jurisdictions where five percent or more of the citizens of voting age belong to a single language-minority group, there must be bilingual voter registration and election materials, as well as other forms of assistance to those for whom English is a second language.

As the late Willie Velasquez, founder and executive director of the Southwest Voter Registration and Education Project, told the conference, the Voting Rights Amendments helped Hispanics increase their participation and power in the political system in the Southwest, often in alliance with blacks and Native Americans. (Regretfully, Mr. Velasquez's essay on Hispanic voting rights, originally planned for inclusion in this volume, was not completed due to his untimely death.)

More Hispanics registered to vote; for instance, in Texas between 1976 and 1980 the number of Mexican-Americans registered to vote in Texas increased from 488,000 to 798,000—or 64 percent. Mexican-Americans and other minorities benefited from the shift from at-large to district-by-district elections for city council members. In 56 communities across the state, Mexican-American and black representation increased from 41 percent to 60 percent.

Another group of language minorities, Asian Americans, has suffered from outbursts of bigotry ranging from the hostility toward Chinese immigrants at the turn of the century to the detention of Japanese-Americans during World War II to the problems facing Vietnamese and Laotian immigrants in today's America.

Chinese immigrants were not allowed to become citizens until 1943 when Congress repealed the Chinese Exclusion Act. As Henry Der, executive director of Chinese for Affirmative Action, told the conference, Asian Americans still face significant obstacles to enfranchisement, despite the 1975 bilingual election amendments. Focusing on California, where more than one-third of all Asian Americans live, and San Francisco, where they are 30 percent of the population, Der contends that Asians have gotten the message that they are "unwelcome" in the political process. Only one-third of all Asian Americans were registered to vote in 1988; no Asian American had ever been elected to the San Francisco Board of Supervisors; and, in 1982, in an extraordinary instance of minority voter harassment, the U.S. Attorney for Northern California launched an investigation of the citizenship status of foreign-born voters requesting bilingual ballots in San Francisco and nine other counties.

Like Asian Americans, Native Americans have also had to fight not only for enfranchisement but even for citizenship. In 1884, in *Elk v. Wilkins*, the Supreme Court ruled that Native Americans were not citizens of the United States—a decision that remained in effect for four decades until Congress passed the Indian Citizenship Act of 1924. While this law enfranchised Native Americans in most

15

states, they did not win the right to vote in Arizona and New Mexico until 1948.

These papers about the barriers to participation by specific demographic groups tell only part of the story of declining voter turnout in today's America—a phenomenon which cuts across lines of race, ethnicity, gender, and generation and may, increasingly, be defined primarily by class.

Even as barriers to voter participation have been torn down, voter turnout has declined steadily over the past three decades— from 62.8 percent of the eligible electorate in the 1960 presidential election to only 50.2 percent in 1988, the lowest level since the election of 1924. Meanwhile, participation in off-year elections is even lower: turnout in the 1986 congressional election was 37 percent, the lowest since 1942 when millions of Americans were overseas fighting World War II.

This problem of declining voter turnout was discussed by several participants in the conference, including Bill Clinton (then governor of Arkansas), who offered two reasons for concern that go beyond the pieties usually presented by civic leaders and editorial writers:

> If we are going to ask our people to endure short term sacrifices for long-term gains, how can they be expected to do so if they haven't been involved in the process of making the decisions through electing candidates and validating and debating the policies to be followed?

> We are going to be more racially and culturally diverse. It will be more difficult to preserve the idea of the United States of America ... We must look at ways to hold our nation together. One clear way of doing that is to have a system in which 80 percent of the people participate on election day, instead of 50 percent.

Clinton, U.S. Senator Alan Cranston, and U.S. Representative John Conyers each discussed proposals before Congress to make it

16

easier for people to register and vote. These proposals, each of which has been tried by various state governments, include:

- Having state motor vehicle agencies register people to vote as they apply for their drivers' licenses.
- Having state human service agencies, including those providing public assistance and unemployment compensation, register voters.
- Allowing voter registration by mail.

In 1992, the Senate and House passed the Motor Voter Registration Bill which would have allowed people to register to vote when they apply for or renew their drivers' licenses as well as when they apply for public services such as welfare and unemployment compensation, marriage licenses or hunting permits. President Bush vetoed the legislation on July 2, 1992.

Four years after the conference was held—and, after yet another presidential election in which turnout declined from the previous one—a fundamental question remains unanswered: Why are fewer and fewer people voting even as more and more barriers to their participation are torn down? This question was posed by the political scientist Ruy Teixeira, in an essay entitled "The Depoliticization of America," in which he notes that the "13 point decline in voter turnout since 1960 has come at a period when registration has actually gotten easier in most states."[2] This is a seeming paradox which in no way lessens the importance of removing the remaining barriers to voter participation but also points up the urgency of motivating non-voters to participate in the system.

In fact, the problem may not be non-participation all across the social spectrum but rather non-participation that is heavily concentrated among Americans of low and moderate incomes. Almost three-quarters of the more affluent Americans vote; more than half of the less affluent do not. As the journalist Robert Kuttner notes, "In the 1980 presidential election, 73.7 percent of people with incomes of $25,000 and over actually voted, but only 48.8 percent

17

of those with incomes between $5,000 and $9,999 cast votes."[3] During the 1980s, "the trend toward increasingly class-skewed voting patterns" increased still further, as the journalist Thomas Edsall has noted,[4] with the exception of the 1982 elections, held in the midst of a national recession that apparently prompted a large protest vote by blue-collar workers, the unemployed, and the poor.

The lesson of the recent past—and, indeed, the lesson of two centuries of American history—may well be that voter participation can be dramatically increased only by building political movements that mobilize the nonparticipants. In the past, voter turnout has been boosted by movements as diverse as the Jacksonian Democrats who mobilized voters from farmers along the frontier to workers in the fast-growing cities; the Populists and the presidential campaign of William Jennings Bryan who mobilized similar constituencies seven decades later; the presidential campaign of Al Smith who dramatically increased the turnout of urban Catholics in 1928; and Franklin Roosevelt's New Deal which increased voter turnout among industrial workers and the poor during the 1930s and 1940s.

More recently, black voter turnout in Chicago increased from 55.4 percent in 1982 (a high level for a mid-term election, resulting, in part, from a voter registration campaign aiming at the next year's mayoral elections) to an extraordinary 70.4 percent in 1983, when Harold Washington was elected mayor. And, during the 1980s, more than 2.5 million black voters registered throughout the nation, particularly in the South, as a result of voter registration campaigns by the Voter Education Project, Operation Big Vote, the A. Philip Randolph Institute, the Coalition of Black Trade Unionists, Project Vote, and Jesse Jackson's Rainbow Coalition and his presidential campaigns of 1984 and 1988. Meanwhile, on the other side of the political spectrum, voter registration among conservative whites, also particularly in the South, was promoted by the Religious Right and Pat Robertson's presidential campaign in 1988.

However, among low and moderate income people who were not mobilized by these various organizations, candidates, and appeals, the politics of the 1980s may have resembled the issueless, passionless, low-turnout elections of the 1920s, when the major parties and their campaigns failed to reach almost half of the eligible electorate of that time. Both periods were marked by a weakened labor movement, relatively uninspiring national candidates in the Democratic Party (which then as now represented many of the constituencies with low voter participation), and a national politics dominated by the wealthy and the business interests.

But the experience of the 1920s also shows that low-participation politics need not be permanent. As Al Smith's unsuccessful presidential campaign demonstrated near the end of that decade, some of those who did not vote in 1920 and 1924 could be mobilized by a campaign that appealed to their ethnic and religious pride and to their desire to be full participants in American life. Later, Franklin Roosevelt's successful presidencies and presidential campaigns revealed that even more of the non-participants of the 1920s could become active participants in the politics of the 1930s and 1940s as a result of a style of leadership, a tangible program, and the creation of such new institutions as the industrial unions, all of which appealed directly to the interests and the values of working people and the poor.

Of course, there are many differences between the decades of the 1920s, 1930s, and 1940s, and our own immediate past and immediate future. Nonetheless, as Martin Luther King suggested in his famous speech at the 1963 March on Washington, it is necessary not only to address those who "cannot vote" but also those who have "nothing for which to vote"—those who, as Al Raby said in this conference, "don't see a relationship between their vote and a change in their own lives, and with good reason." Now, in the 1990s, it may still be possible—and the future of American democracy may depend upon that possibility—to build political movements that motivate and mobilize low and moderate income people, black and white and Hispanic, and convince them that their votes can bring about "a change in their own lives." Such movements could expand the electorate in our own time, just as the movements led by Andrew Jackson, Al Smith, and Franklin Roosevelt all did in the past.

Appropriately, two of the speakers at the conference—each of whom died before his time, just several months after this conference—exemplify the kind of activism that can motivate and mobilize those who have been shut out or turned off by the political system.

Al Raby was a veteran of more than a quarter century of civil rights and community activism in Chicago, as a leader in the school integration efforts of the early 1960s, an aide to Martin Luther King during his "war on slums" in 1965 and 1966, and as manager of Harold Washington's mayoral campaign in 1983. Raby was chairman of the board of Project Vote, Inc., an organization which "pioneer[ed] the strategy of registering voters in welfare offices, food stamp, unemployment, and cheese lines—all of the places where the poor are made to wait to receive 'services' from an uncaring economy and government." Raby attacked the myths that poor people cannot be registered, and that, once registered, they won't vote. What is essential, Raby argued, is that their political participation continue past election day as part of a continuing effort to address real-life issues like housing, education, and job opportunities.

As founder and president of the Southwest Voter Registration Education Project, Willie Velasquez helped to register more than a million new Hispanic voters. Using the motto "Su voto es su voz" ("Your vote is your voice"), Velasquez persuaded people that voting was the way to win a better life. As he explained:

> The tradition in the vast majority of Southwestern cities is that the Mexican side of town is not paved, much less provided adequate municipal services, and the schools in our side of town are terribly inferior. Better municipal services and better schools consistently rank as the top two priorities in all our work in the field and in our polls.

The life's work of Willie Velasquez and Al Raby is the most

20

eloquent testimonial to the message of this book: that American democracy can—and must—be expanded by expanding the American electorate. It is a message that is even more urgent now than when these papers were presented.

NOTES

1. Frances Fox Piven and Richard Cloward, *Why Americans Don't Vote* (New York: Pantheon Books, 1989), pp. 30, 54.

2. Ruy A. Teixeira, "The Depoliticization of America," *The Commonwealth Report*, September 1989, p. 5.

3. Robert Kuttner, *The Life of the Party: Democratic Prospects in 1988 and Beyond* (New York: Viking Books, 1987), p. 124.

4. Thomas B. Edsall, *The New Politics of Inequality* (New York: Norton, 1984), p. 191.

The Constitution
and the
Franchise

The constitutions of Georgia and South Carolina contained explicit provisions limiting suffrage to "white males." Colonies prohibited voting by such diverse groups as strangers, drunks, former criminals, servants, women, Indians, Catholics, Jews, and Negroes.

The Struggle to Gain the Right to Vote: 1787-1965

Karen McGill Arrington

From colonial times to the framing of the Constitution, from the Civil War and its aftermath to the civil rights struggles of our own era, no issue has been more fundamental to American politics than the question of who should have the right to participate in the political system. Over the past two centuries, the system has evolved from exclusion to inclusion, as, one by one, the most egregious barriers to political participation have been torn down.

The Colonial Period

At the time of the Revolutionary War, a few freed black men who could meet the property requirements in the northern colonies voted along with white men. In Virginia and North Carolina, no "negro, mulatto, or Indian could vote."[1] And the constitutions of Georgia and South Carolina contained explicit provisions limiting suffrage to "white males."[2] Colonies prohibited voting by such diverse groups as strangers, drunks, former criminals, servants, women, Indians, Catholics, Jews, and Negroes.

Women were allowed to vote in Massachusetts from 1691 to 1780. From 1776 to 1806, New Jersey permitted women over the age of 21 to vote if they had fulfilled a one-year residency and owned property with a value of at least 50 pounds.[3] This right was repealed in 1806, and in 1807 the state legislature inserted "white male" in the statute.[4]

25

Roman Catholics were not allowed to vote in most of the American colonies; Jews were denied the ballot in New York and South Carolina. Massachusetts and New Jersey required that freed men be church members in order to vote. Quakers were not allowed to vote in some New England states, and their religious bar against taking oaths excluded them from the ballot in their colonies.[5]

As the push for white male suffrage grew, spurred on by the young men who had served in the Revolutionary War, many states that had permitted freed black men to enjoy the franchise, among them New Jersey, Pennsylvania, and Connecticut, now moved to disenfranchise them.

The Constitutional Convention

When the founding fathers met in Philadelphia in May 1787, many were concerned about the movement to liberalize the franchise. New Hampshire, Pennsylvania, Vermont, and Georgia had eliminated the requirement that voters be landowners. Vermont had the most liberal law: Every adult male was automatically eligible to vote and could be elected to office. Such voting reforms had been set in motion during the Revolutionary War with the enlistment of young men, most of whom at that time could not vote because they had not acquired property of any value.

According to author Bill Severn in *The Right to Vote*, Alexander Hamilton told the Constitutional Convention, "The people seldom judge or determine right."[6] Severn noted that Hamilton "thought the time had come to create a strong national government that would be largely protected from 'an excess of democracy' and from the 'violence and turbulence of the democratic spirit.' Hamilton recommended having the nation's president and senators hold office for life instead of for short terms and he wanted them chosen indirectly by men who were lifetime owners of land."[7]

The Convention delegates agreed that the president and the Senate would be protected from the direct vote of the people. The president was to be chosen by the votes of state electors appointed "in such Manner as the Legislator thereof may direct." [8] The senators were to be chosen by the members of the state legislature.[9] The House of Representatives was to be chosen by the direct vote of the people; the question, then, was who would be eligible to vote for these representatives.

Many of the delegates wanted a constitutional provision limiting the right to vote to landholders. A committee was established to draft national voting requirements that would take into consideration the liberal franchise laws of some of the states. But, as it was impossible to establish requirements that would not disenfranchise persons already given the right to vote by some states, and, at the same time, adhere to the limitations of other states, the committee recommended that voting qualifications be left to the individual states. This recommendation was adopted because it was believed that states would not ratify the Constitution if it took away recently won voting rights.[10]

According to Article 1, Section 4, of the Constitution, the states were given the authority to determine who was eligible to vote and to regulate the "times, places and manner of holding elections for Senators and Representatives," but Congress had the authority "at any time by law [to] make or alter such Regulations, except as to the Places of chusing Senators."

Thus the Constitution, by leaving voting requirements to the states, allowed for continued diversity in voting rights among the states and for the disenfranchisement of segments of the society. (There is no reason to believe national requirements would have been any less restrictive.) But at the same time, by giving Congress the authority to alter state regulations, the Constitution handed the federal government the right to judge elections. Two centuries later, this authority would be used to expand the right to vote.

Exclusion of Minorities and Women

By the mid-1800s, blacks were almost totally disenfranchised throughout the states. Northern freed black men who had managed

27

to acquire property had lost the right to vote; moreover, as state constitutions were amended to liberalize voting for non-owners of land, the words "white male" were inserted.[11] Between 1792 and 1838 the constitutions of Connecticut, Delaware, Kentucky, Maryland, New Jersey, North Carolina, Tennessee, and Virginia were changed to exclude all Negroes from voting, despite their proclamations of equal rights for all men.[12]

Few blacks were able to participate in the political process in the nineteenth century. In *Race, Racism and American Law*, Professor Derrick Bell described the prevailing conditions and attitudes:

> By 1840, some 93 percent of the northern free Negro population lived in States which completely or practically excluded them from the right to vote. Only in Massachusetts, New Hampshire, Vermont and Maine could Negroes vote on an equal basis with whites. In New York, they could vote if they first met property and residence requirements. In New Jersey, Pennsylvania, and Connecticut, they were completely disfranchised, after having once enjoyed the ballot.

In several states the adoption of white manhood suffrage led directly to the political disfranchisement of the Negroes. Those who opposed an expanded electorate for both whites and Negroes warned that it would, among other things, grant the Negro political power. Adopt universal manhood suffrage, a Pennsylvania constitutional convention delegate declared in 1837, and "every negro in the State, worthy and worthless, degraded and debased, as nine tenths of them are, will rush to the polls in senseless and unmeaning triumph."[13]

From 1800 until the Civil War, every state that was admitted to the Union except Maine restricted the franchise to whites.[14] By the time of the Civil War, only in Maine, New Hampshire, Vermont, Rhode Island, and Massachusetts were freed blacks allowed to vote, and the blacks in these states comprised only six percent of the nation's black population. While Maine entered the union allowing

28

blacks to vote, very few blacks resided there. Maine officials were concerned about the state's larger Indian population, and Maine's constitution of 1819 did not permit Indians to vote unless they were taxpayers.[15]

Between 1788, when the U.S. Constitution was ratified, and the late 1800s, when the "Civil War Amendments" were enacted, women voted in a few states. Kentucky allowed women to vote in local elections beginning in 1838; Kansas women voted in school elections for the first time in 1861; Wyoming, as a territory, allowed women to vote in 1869; and Colorado's constitution of 1876 permitted women to vote in school elections.[16]

Ratification of the Thirteenth, Fourteenth, and Fifteenth Amendments to the Constitution, the Civil War Amendments, was the beginning of the struggle to gain the right to vote for blacks, other minorities, and women—a struggle that continues today.

Blacks' Struggle to Gain Voting Rights

Following the Civil War, Congress passed the Thirteenth, Fourteenth, and Fifteenth Amendments in order to eradicate slavery and to establish legal rights for the newly emancipated slaves. The Fifteenth Amendment prohibits states from denying the right to vote on the basis of "race, color, or previous condition of servitude." An earlier version that failed to gain Congressional approval sought universal manhood suffrage, i.e., suffrage regardless of education or land ownership. Senator Henry Wilson of Massachusetts introduced a draft text that prohibited restricting the right to vote on the basis of race, color, creed, nativity, property, or education. This provision passed the Senate but was amended in compromise with the House.[17]

The Fifteenth Amendment was ratified with great difficulty. Southern states were required to ratify it as a condition for readmission to the Union, and ultimately it would not have been ratified without their support. New York passed, then rescinded, the amendment; California, Delaware, Kentucky, Maryland, Oregon, and Tennessee

29

rejected it.[18] The amendment was finally ratified by the requisite number of states in 1870.

— Southern blacks experienced a brief period of political participation following ratification of the Fifteenth Amendment, but soon a movement erupted to disenfranchise blacks again. Between 1890 and 1910, 12 states acted to make the franchise totally white through measures that, though racially neutral on their face, resulted in almost total disenfranchisement for blacks. The most common measures used were literacy tests and poll taxes. In Louisiana, blacks had constituted 44 percent of the electorate following the Civil War, yet in 1920 they comprised less than one percent of the voting population. In Mississippi in 1867, almost 70 percent of the blacks of voting age were registered; but by 1892, two years after voting requirements seeking to end black political participation went into effect, less than six percent of blacks of voting age were registered.[19]

Illiterate whites, it should be noted, were provided alternatives that allowed them to vote despite these measures; for example, the "grandfather clause" stipulating that no lineal descendent of any person qualified to vote on January 1, 1866, should be denied the right to vote.[20] Although some devices to restrict voting by blacks were struck down by the courts, others, including poll taxes and literacy tests, survived. The civil rights laws enacted after the Civil War were interpreted narrowly by the courts. —

From 1871 to 1957, not one new piece of federal civil rights legislation was enacted. In 1957 Congress passed the Civil Rights Act of 1957, giving the U.S. Attorney General authority to institute suits on behalf of blacks who were denied the right to vote. The act also directed that a U.S. Commission on Civil Rights be created to investigate complaints alleging that citizens have been denied the right to vote by reason of their race, color, religion, or national origin. Civil rights laws passed in 1960 and 1964 strengthened the 1957 law but brought about little progress in black voting.

A major breakthrough occurred when the Voting Rights Act of

1965 was passed. This act suspended literacy tests in many areas of the country and provided for direct action by the federal government to enable blacks to register and vote. Now court challenges were not the only avenue available to gain the franchise for blacks.[21] The Voting Rights Act was expanded and extended in 1970, 1975, and 1982.[22]

The Voting Rights Act has been hailed as perhaps the nation's most effective civil rights legislation. It has allowed large numbers of blacks to register and vote, and it has led to the election of numerous black officials. More than half of the country's 6,800 black elected officials are in jurisdictions subject to provisions of the Voting Rights Act.[23]

Women's Suffrage

To a great extent, the women's movement grew out of the abolitionist movement. Women leaders expected that when blacks gained the right to vote, women would be included.[24] When this did not occur, some turned their attention to the states and focused on passage of a federal suffrage provision. Between 1866 and 1918, numerous measures were introduced in Congress to grant women the right to vote. All of them failed. As Professor Mary Frances Berry wrote in *Why ERA Failed*:

> In 1866, Republican Senator Samuel C. Pomeroy of Kansas presented a proposed suffrage bill to the Senate, and Indiana Congressman George W. Jullian presented a joint resolution on the subject to both houses in 1869. Both proposals died without a vote being taken. Twelve resolutions to extend suffrage to women were introduced between 1875 and 1888 in the Congress. Usually they were reported back to the committee to which they had been referred, with extended reports from the majority and the minority. In 1878, Senator A.A. Sargent of California, a friend of Susan B. Anthony, introduced. . .the Anthony amendment ["The right of

31

citizens of the United States to vote shall not be denied or abridged by the United States or any state on account of sex."], which is the text of the Nineteenth Amendment as finally passed by Congress. After hearings, Sargent's proposal was reported adversely back to committee. In 1887, a women's suffrage amendment gained a vote on the Senate floor, but lost 34-14. Twenty-two of the opposing senators were from the South. In 1888, Mason of Illinois unsuccessfully attempted to give "widows and spinsters" the right to vote on the rationale that they had no male voter to represent their interest.[25]

The Nineteenth Amendment was not brought to the Senate floor for another vote until March 17, 1914, when it failed by a vote of 35 to 34, far short of the necessary two-thirds.[26] The House voted on the amendment for the first time on January 12, 1915, and defeated it by a vote of 204 to 174.[27]

Nevertheless, suffrage for women was gaining support in some states. When Wyoming entered the Union in 1890, it already allowed women to vote;[28] the Wyoming legislature had passed a suffrage bill in 1869.[29] Other Western states followed suit: Colorado in 1893, Utah and Idaho in 1896.[30] On June 4, 1919, when the Nineteenth Amendment was passed by Congress, some 20 states had already granted women the right to vote.[31]

With many states already having granted women the right to vote, ratification of the Nineteenth Amendment was expected to occur quickly. Wisconsin was the first state to ratify the measure, and within two months of passage by Congress, 14 states had approved it. The pace of ratification slowed, but on August 26, 1920, Tennessee became the thirty-sixth state to ratify the amendment, and the proclamation granting women the right to vote was signed that same day.[32]

From the time the Nineteenth Amendment was ratified until the 1940s, women registered and voted at a rate much below that of men. To a great extent this was due to attitudinal factors, including a widely held view that participation in political matters was inconsistent with the woman's traditional role of homemaker. During World War II this attitude began to change as women entered the work force in unprecedented numbers. However, until the 1980s, the rate for women still lagged behind that for men by at least 10 percentage points. The turnout of women in the 1984 presidential election "exceeded that of men for the first time...."[33]

The Treatment of Asians

According to archaeological evidence, Asians migrated to this continent some 40,000 to 100,000 years ago.[34] If one considers the years after Columbus landed in this hemisphere, the presence of Asian settlers on this continent can be documented as far back as 1763, and in the United States as early as 1785, but it was not until the 1940s that Asian immigrants were allowed to become citizens through naturalization.[35] The adoption of the Fourteenth Amendment made any children born in the United States citizens without respect to the status of their parents.

The first major labor-related Chinese immigration to the United States began in the mid-1800s when Chinese working men were brought to Hawaii to work on the sugarcane and pineapple plantations. Male Chinese were later brought to the mainland to work on the railroads and in the mines. Japanese Americans arrived at the turn of this century as seasonal migrant agricultural workers in California and Hawaii.[36]

The Naturalization Act of 1790 provided that "any alien being a free White person" could apply for naturalization; after the Civil War the law was changed to permit naturalization of persons of African descent as well. But federal law did not grant the same privilege to Asian immigrants. Some states (e.g., Indiana, Kansas, Wisconsin) that needed settlers and workers gave aliens the right to vote as an inducement for them to relocate.[37] There is no indication, however, that this offer was extended to Asians.

A nationwide recession during the 1870s caused serious labor problems on the West Coast, and Chinese workers became the target of harassment and violence. Congress passed the Chinese Exclusion Act of 1882, which prohibited the entrance of Chinese laborers into the country for 10 years "except for those who were in the country on November 17, 1880"; the act also prevented Chinese immigrants already here from attaining citizenship.[38] This act was extended for 10 years in 1892, for 2 years in 1902, and indefinitely in 1904 (although it was later repealed).[39]

Around the turn of the century, Japanese immigrants replaced the Chinese as a source of cheap labor. In 1907 a "gentlemen's agreement" between the United States and Japan provided that Japan would not issue passports to "skilled or unskilled "laborers not previously in the United States.[40] Congress further limited the immigration of the Japanese in 1917 by creating an "Asia-Pacific Triangle, an Asiatic barred zone, designed to exclude Asians completely from immigration to the United States."[41]

Another exclusion act instituted in 1924 completely ended the immigration of Asians except for Filipinos, who were subjects of the United States. But in 1925 legislation was enacted that declared Filipinos ineligible for citizenship unless they served three years in the U.S. Navy.

The 1924 National Origins Act "prohibited the immigration of aliens ineligible for citizenship, completely clos[ing] the door on Japanese immigration."[42] The Supreme Court had ruled in 1922 in *Takao Ozawa* v. *United States* [43] that persons of Japanese ancestry could not become naturalized citizens.[44]

Chinese immigrants were not allowed to gain citizenship until 1943, when Congress repealed the Chinese Exclusion Act and allowed 105 Chinese to immigrate annually.[45] Legislation enacted in 1946 granted "eligibility for naturalization to Filipinos and to races indigenous to India."[46]

By passing the Walter-McCarran Act in 1952, Congress "removed the bar to immigration and citizenship for races that had been denied those privileges prior to that time."[47] While Asian immigrants still had to endure discriminatory quotas, they were granted the right to become citizens and, thus, the right to vote. The National Origins Act's immigration quotas were abolished in 1965.

The Struggle of Native Americans

Although Native Americans have inhabited this land for perhaps 50,000 years, they were not made citizens by virtue of birth in the United States until 1924.

In 1884 in *Elk* v. *Wilkins*,[48] the Supreme Court ruled that Native Americans were not made citizens under the Fourteenth Amendment. In 1887 Congress passed the General Allotment Act (also known as the Dawes Act), which "set the pattern for allotting Indian reservations. Each family head was to receive 160 acres, and a single person was to receive 80 acres. Title to the land was to be held in trust for at least 25 years."[49] The act also conferred citizenship on Native Americans who disassociated themselves from the tribe.

The Indian Naturalization Act of 1890 allowed tribal members to become citizens, but they had to apply for citizenship in the same manner as did immigrants. The Indian Citizenship Act of 1924 declared that Native Americans born in the United States were citizens.[50]

In Arizona and New Mexico, Native Americans could not vote until 1948.[51] States have tried to prevent Native Americans from voting by making the following assertions:

- Reservation residents are not residents of the states in which the reservation is located.
- Indians are wards of the federal government.
- Because they are "not taxed," they are not entitled to a voice in state or city politics.[52]

Denial of Rights to Hispanics

While Mexicans who remained in the "conquered Southwest" following the United States victory in the Mexican War of 1848 were guaranteed full citizenship by the Treaty of Guadalupe, the exercise of the franchise did not come quite so easily for many Hispanics. English proficiency requirements limited the voting rights of many Hispanics and were not addressed nationally until the Voting Rights Act amendments of 1975 were passed. As a result of testimony provided to Congress in 1975:

> Congress found that because of the denial of equal educational opportunities by State and local governments, language minorities experienced severe disabilities and illiteracy in the English language that, together with English-only elections, excluded them from participation in the electoral process. Congress, therefore, determined that to enforce the 14th and 15th amendments to the U.S. Constitution, it was "necessary to eliminate such discrimination by prohibiting English-only elections and by prescribing other remedial devices."[53]

A report of the California Advisory Committee to the U.S. Commission on Civil Rights entitled "Political Participation of Mexican Americans in California" stated that many of the methods used in the past to exclude Mexican Americans from political participation in California were strikingly similar to those used to exclude blacks from political participation in the South.[54]

Such methods included "tests based on education and literacy, gerrymandering of voting districts and intimidation; and, on occasion, murder."[55] The South had its poll taxes and grandfather clauses to discourage the black vote; California had its English-language voting requirements and threats of deportation to discourage the Mexican American voter.[56]

Focus on the Franchise

The Leadership Conference Education Fund believes that the study of American history and politics should include an examination of how countless American citizens have been denied the promise of the Constitution and how our nation has struggled for two centuries to include them in that promise. By focusing on the franchise, we are in effect inspecting the heart of the Constitution. Eight of the 16 amendments since ratification of the Bill of Rights address the issue of voting, seeking to bring more Americans into the political process. The "remaking" of the Constitution over the last 200 years says much about our country and helps illuminate what remains to be accomplished.

Notes

1. Cortlandt F. Bishop, *History of Elections in the American Colonies* (New York: Columbia College, 1893), p. 51.

2. Report of the U.S. Commission on Civil Rights, 1959, p. 25.

3. Mary Frances Berry, *Why E.R.A. Failed: Politics, Women's Rights and the Amending Process of the Constitution* (Bloomington: Indiana University Press, 1986), p. 30.

4. *Ibid.*; Leslie Friedman Goldstein, *The Constitutional Rights of Women, Cases in Law and Social Change* (New York: Longman, 1979).

5. Report of the U.S. Commission on Civil Rights, 1959, p. 21.

6. As quoted in Bill Severn, *The Right to Vote* (New York: Washburn, 1972), p. 20.

7. Alexander Hamilton, in Severn, *The Right to Vote*.

8. Article 2, Section 1, of the U.S. Constitution.

9. Article 1, Section 3, of the U.S. Constitution.

10. Severn, *The Right to Vote*, pp. 23-24.

11. Derrick A. Bell, Jr., *Race, Racism and American Law* (Boston: Little, Brown and Co., 1973), p. 120.

12. Severn, *The Right to Vote*, p. 85.

13. Bell, *Race, Racism and American Law*, p. 119-20.

14. Severn, *The Right to Vote*, p. 85.

15. *Ibid.*, p.31; Marchette Chute, *The First Liberty: A History of the Right To Vote* (New York: E.P. Dupont and Co., Inc., 1969), p. 312.

16. Report of the U.S. Commission on Civil Rights, 1959, p. 25.

17. Jack Bass, "Election Laws and Their Manipulation to Exclude Minority Voters," in Rockefeller Foundation, *The Right to Vote* (New York: October 1981), p. 2.

18. Bell, *Race, Racism and American Law*, p. 121.

19. U.S. Commission on Civil Rights, "Voting in Mississippi" (Washington, D.C.: GPO, 1965), p. 5.

20. Bell, *Race, Racism and American Law*, pp. 123-24.

21. U.S. Commission on Civil Rights, "Political Participation" (Washington: GPO, 1968), pp. 10-11.

22. In 1982 the major provisions of the bill were extended until 2007, with the exception of Section 203 (bilingual requirements), which was extended for 10 years and will expire in August 1992. Efforts are now under way to extend this bilingual provision until 2007 as well.

23. Joint Center for Political and Economic Studies, *Black Elected Officials: A National Roster* (Washington, D.C.: Joint Center, 1987), p. 1. It is worth noting that while the Fifteenth Amendment prohibits all states from denying the right to vote on the basis of race, the Voting Rights Act has some special requirements for states with a history of discrimination in voting (i.e., states that circumvented the Fifteenth Amendment by using discriminatory techniques).

24. Berry, *Why ERA Failed*, p. 31.

25. *Ibid.*, p. 33.

26. Severn, *The Right to Vote*, p. 76.

27. *Ibid.*, p. 77.

28. Citizens' Commission on Civil Rights, "Barriers to Registration and Voting: An Agenda for Reform" (Washington, D.C.: National Center for Policy Alternatives, 1988), p. 31.

29. Berry, *Why Era Failed*, p. 35.

30. Severn, *The Right to Vote*, p. 72.

31. *Ibid.*, p. 83; U.S. Department of Commerce, Bureau of the Census, "Historical Statistics of the United States: Colonial Times to 1957" (Washington, D.C.: GPO, 1961).

32. Severn, *The Right to Vote*, p. 83.

33. Citizens' Commission on Civil Rights, "Barriers to Registration," III-36.

34. U.S. Commission on Civil Rights, "Indian Tribes: A Continuing Quest for Survival" (Washington, D.C.: GPO, 1981), p. 15.

35. Pacific/Asian American Mental Health Research Center, *Political Participation of Asian Americans: Problems and Strategies*, Yung-Hwan Jo (ed.) (Chicago: 1980), p. 16.

36. U.S. Commission on Civil Rights, "Issues of Asian and Pacific Americans: Myths and Realities" (Washington, D.C.: GPO, 1979), p. 5.

37. Report of the U.S. Commission on Civil Rights, 1959, p. 25.

38. U.S. Commission on Civil Rights, "The Tarnished Golden Door: Civil Rights Issues in Immigration" (Washington, D.C.: GPO, September 1980), p. 8.

39. *Ibid.*, p. 8.

40. *Ibid.*, p. 8.

41. *Ibid.*, p. 9. Note that exemptions were made for persons from Persia and parts of Afghanistan and Russia.

42. U.S. Commission on Civil Rights, "The Tarnished Golden Door," p. 9.

43. 260 U.S. 173.

44. U.S. Commission on Civil Rights, "The Tarnished Golden Door," p. 10.

45. *Ibid.*, p. 10.

46. *Ibid.*, p. 10.

47. *Ibid.*, p. 11.

48. 112 U.S. 94.

49. U.S. Commission on Civil Rights, "Indian Tribes," 21.

50. *Ibid.*, p. 21.

51. Citizens' Commission on Civil Rights, "Barriers to Registration," III-25.

52. U.S. Commission on Civil Rights, *American Indian Civil Rights Handbook* (Washington, D.C.: GPO, 1972), p. 57.

53. U.S. Commission on Civil Rights, "The Voting Rights Act: Unfulfilled Goals" (Washington, D.C.: GPO, 1981), p. 77.

54. California Advisory Committee to the U.S. Commission on Civil Rights, "Political Participation of Mexican Americans in California" (Washington, D.C.: GPO, 1971), p. 5.

55. *Ibid.*, p. 5.

56. *Ibid.*, p. 5.

Even today, in the late twentieth century, we still feel the reverberations of the compromise struck at the Constitutional Convention 200 years ago. The exclusion of blacks from the document, the nod given to enslavement, the degradation of blacks as less than "whole" human beings—all these factors set the stage for the racial hatred that colors the actions of today's Ku Klux Klan; that erupts into the ugliness of Forsyth County, Georgia, and Howard Beach, New York; that results in the devastating statistics on today's black families.

A Promise Yet Unfulfilled

Judge Damon J. Keith

During the formative years of colonial America, blacks were permitted to vote. Yet the idea of granting the franchise permanently to blacks incited heated debate less than a century later at the Constitutional Convention in Philadelphia. It is imperative, therefore, that we analyze this early phase of our nation's history and its ramifications for our society.

A promise was made in Philadelphia: that "We the People"— all of us—are "endowed with certain inalienable rights, including life, liberty and the pursuit of happiness." But after 200 years it is a promise unfulfilled for black Americans.[1] Any discussion of the franchise must deal with the issue of slavery, for the two go hand in hand: If one is a slave, naturally one is not free. And if one is not free, one cannot vote. At least that's the way it was in colonial America.

The Franchise During the Colonial Period

The first known record of blacks arriving in an American colony was in 1619, when the secretary and recorder of the Virginia Colony, John Rolfe, noted that "a Dutchman sold the Governor and Cape Marchand twenty Negroes."[2] These Africans arrived in Jamestown a year before the first Pilgrims landed at Plymouth Rock! They had been bought as captives, of course, from Dutchmen who had seized them from a Spanish ship.

In 1619, however, there was no legal framework into which to

43

fit this new race of people. Consequently, the first generation of blacks had much more freedom than American blacks would later have. In fact, blacks in the earliest period actually voted and participated in public life. It was not until 1723 that blacks were denied the right to vote in Virginia; 1721 in South Carolina; 1715 in North Carolina; and 1754 in Georgia.[3] Not only did these early blacks vote, but they also held public office. For example, there was a "black surety" in New York County, Virginia, in the first decades of the seventeenth century.[4] Moreover, when they first arrived in America, blacks were often assigned the status of indentured servants, not slaves. This is an important distinction, because there was a major chasm between the status of "servant" and that of "slave." Servants were indentured workers freed after working a set number of years. Indentured servants often were European immigrants who bought their passage to America in exchange for years of their labor. Slaves, on the other hand, were doomed to lifelong servitude with no hope of earning freedom except by escaping. The notion of treating blacks as indentured servants and not slaves soon changed, however, as laws began to emerge that would institutionalize the degradation of blacks.

While courts' decisions were often erratic with respect to precisely defining the legal status of blacks during the colonial period, legislatures were quick to take up the slack. Within 20 years of the first arrival of Africans in 1619 in Jamestown, the Virginia Colonial Council began to write laws that excluded blacks:

> 1639 Act X. All persons except Negroes are to be provided with arms and ammunition or be fined at the pleasure of the governor and council.[5]

Later statutes dealt with runaway servants: In 1658, a statute required that all masters, upon apprehending their runaways, "cut the hair of all such runaways close above the ears, whereby they may be with more ease discovered and apprehended [in the future]."[6] The fear of rebellion by servants, both black and white, was also on the minds of legislators. The penalties for any English servant who ran away in the company of any Negro was to make the English servant a lifelong slave, just like the Negro slave.[7]

Obviously, to deter slaves from running away, there was little available in the way of threats (such as lengthening time of service) except the specter of death or serious bodily harm. The threat of death was the slaveholder's most powerful tool against runaways, but slaveholders feared that if they beat their slaves too severely, they might be guilty of violating criminal laws of battery or murder. Thus, in 1669, the Virginia Legislature passed a statute to notify slaveholders that if they killed a slave during a beating, they would not be prosecuted.[8]

The first major slave codes in Virginia were dated 1680 to 1682.[9] The 1680 Virginia statute would become the model slave code throughout the South for the next 180 years. This is an example of its codified repression:

> 1680 Act X. Whereas the frequent meetings of considerable numbers of Negro slaves under pretense of feasts and burials is judged of dangerous consequence, [be it] enacted that no Negro or slave may carry arms, such as any club, staff, gun, sword, or other weapon, nor go from his owner's plantation without a certificate and then only on necessary occasions; the punishment twenty lashes on the bare back, well laid on. And further, if any Negro lift up his hand against any Christian he shall receive thirty lashes, and if he absent himself or lie out from his master's service and resist lawful apprehension, he may be killed and this law shall be published every six months.[10]

By the mid-eighteenth century, then, the relative freedom of blacks during the early colonial period had been curbed dramatically. Black slaves were property and simply had no vote. The emancipation of some black slaves concerned the colonies that allowed all free men to vote; in those colonies, freed blacks became victims of increased racial hatred by whites. "The attack waged against free

Blacks was of great importance in New York where, since 1777, all free men, subject to property requirements that were applicable to all regardless of previous conditions of servitude, race, or creed, were able to vote."[11] By 1815 a Republican-controlled New York State Legislature had already passed a bill requiring blacks to obtain special permits in order to vote in state elections.[12] In 1822 the New York State Constitution was amended to abolish the property requirement for white voters; the property requirement for blacks, on the other hand, was increased from $100 to $200.

In Massachusetts, the debate over giving the vote to black free men took place as towns voted on ratification of Article V of the state's proposed constitution in 1778. That article said, in part:

> Every male inhabitant of any town in this state, being free, and twenty-one years of age, excepting Negroes, Indians and Mulattoes, shall be entitled to vote for a Representative or Representatives . . .[13]

This article was rejected by a margin of five to one, and instead a Declaration of Rights was incorporated into the Massachusetts Constitution calling for unqualified male suffrage, for blacks and whites alike.[14]

In the South Carolina colony, however, the situation was much different. Free blacks there could not vote because of a statute passed in 1721 to limit the right of suffrage to "every free white man . . . professing the Christian religion" who also met the age and property requirements.[15]

Thus, the franchise during the colonial period was nonexistent for slaves; it was extended to free blacks in a few rare colonies; and, when not restricted only to white men, it was usually coupled with a fine or property requirement. The debate in Philadelphia at the Constitutional Convention did little to improve this grim situation.

The Debate Over Slavery and the Franchise During the Constitutional Convention

In 1857 U.S. Supreme Court Chief Justice Roger B. Taney, rendering his interpretation of the Declaration of Independence as it applied to blacks, wrote that the words "all men are created equal"

> would seem to embrace the whole human family, and if they were used in a similar instrument at this day would be so understood. But it is too clear for dispute, that the enslaved, African race were not intended to be included, and formed no part of the people who framed and adopted this declaration.... The men who framed this declaration ... knew that it would not in any part of the civilized world be supposed to embrace the Negro race, which, by common consent, had been excluded from civilized governments and the family of nations, and doomed to slavery . . . .[16]

While no one can quarrel with the moral repugnance of the Dred Scott decision from which this quote is extracted, Chief Justice Taney was correct about one thing: The Constitution was not adopted with the Negro race in mind.

Over the 200 years since the Constitutional Convention, the essential focus of those who were "left out" in Philadelphia has been the Preamble of the Constitution, which begins with the stirring words "We the People." The phrase "We the People," taken literally, encompasses all of us. It does not mean "We the White Men." It means every American, black or white, yellow or red, woman or man. "We the People" was a noble, expansive, and tantalizing appetizer to the main course: the Constitution.

Yet the Constitution itself retracted those very words. Perhaps the most cogent statement concerning "We the People" was made by former U.S. Representative Barbara Jordan:

> We the people. It's a very eloquent beginning. But when that document was completed on the 17th of September in 1787, I was not included in that "We the People." I felt

47

somehow for many years that George Washington and Alexander Hamilton just left me out by mistake.[17] But it was not a mistake: Blacks and women were intentionally left out. The debate—and the promise—began and ended over the issue of slavery.

The key question discussed during the Constitutional Convention in 1787 was not really whether slavery should be abolished. The North already had compromised on that issue by conceding the existence of slavery so the South would agree to become a party to the Union. The question instead was: Who should have the power to control slavery—the national government or the states? The compromises the convention delegates reached were (1) that slaves would be counted, for purposes of representation and taxes, in the proportion of five slaves to three white inhabitants—the federal ratio, otherwise known as the "three-fifths rule,"[18] and (2) that the importation of slaves would cease in the year 1808.[19] It was a compromise that was to brand the Negro race for two centuries.

Much of the debate centered on the issue of "proportionality." John Rutledge of South Carolina suggested that the proportional vote in the House be rationed according to the "quotas of contribution"—which meant according to the taxes paid and the amount each state contributed to the national treasury. South Carolina's Pierce Butler agreed, stating that since "money is power," states should have weight in the government proportional to their wealth.

But if taxation was to be the basis for representation, Elbridge Gerry of Massachusetts asked, then what about the slaves? "Blacks are property," he continued, "and are used to the southward as horses and cattle to the northward," hence, why not allow the North to count their horses and cattle for representation?[20]

This question was resolved by the pernicious three-fifths rule, which required that the vote be in proportion to the "whole number of white and other free citizens and three-fifths of all other persons except Indians not paying taxes. ..." The "all other persons" were, of course, slaves. The actual term "slaves," however, was carefully excised from the Constitution, although the three-fifths rule remained the law of the land until the Fourteenth Amendment was passed in 1868.

Thus, the convention delegates did not even contemplate blacks' or women's suffrage. Blacks and women were important only in terms of a state's proportional representation and taxation. The slavery issue was crucial only to strike a compromise to keep the Southern states in the Union. The franchise was, quite simply, not an issue.

In his recent, wonderful book *And We Are Not Saved*, Harvard Professor Derrick Bell recounts the "Chronicle of the Constitutional Contradiction." In his chronicle, Geneva Crenshaw, a black woman from this century, travels back 200 years to the Philadelphia Convention to debate the issue of slavery with the delegates. Imagine for a moment that you are at that convention in Philadelphia. Imagine a hot, crowded room full of ruffled white men. Imagine that a tall black woman suddenly appears in twentieth-century dress. She begins to speak to the clearly shocked and angry delegates. The following exchange is an excerpt from Derrick Bell's "Chronicle,"[21] in the first-person voice of Geneva Crenshaw:

"Gentlemen," I began, "delegates," then paused and, with a slight smile, added, "fellow citizens, I, like some of you, am a Virginian, my forefathers having labored on the land holdings of your fellow patriot, the Honorable Thomas Jefferson. I have come to urge that, in your great work, here, you not restrict the sweep of Mr. Jefferson's self-evident truths that all men are equal and endowed by the Creator with inalienable rights, including 'Life, Liberty and the pursuit of Happiness.' " It was, I thought, a clever touch to invoke the name of Thomas Jefferson who, then serving as American minister to France, was not a member of the Virginia Delegation. But my remark could not overcome the offense of my presence.

49

"How dare you insert yourself in these deliberations?" a delegate demanded.

"I dare," I said, "because slavery is an evil that Jefferson, himself a slave owner and unconvinced that Africans are equal to whites, nevertheless found involved 'a perpetual exercise of the most boisterous passions, the most unremitting despotism of the one part, and degrading submissions on the other.' Slavery, Jefferson has written, brutalizes slave owner as well as slave and, worse of all, tends to undermine the 'only firm basis' of liberty, the conviction in the minds of the people that liberty is 'the gift of God'. . ."

There was a hush in the group. No one wanted to admit it, but the ambivalence on the slavery issue expressed by Jefferson obviously had meaning for at least some of those in the hall. . . .

"The stark truth is that the racial grief that persists today [in the twentieth century]," I ended, "originated in the slavery institutionalized in the document you are drafting. Is this, gentlemen, an achievement for which you wish to be remembered?"

Oblivious to my plea, a delegate tried what he likely considered a sympathetic approach. "Geneva, be reasonable. Go and leave us to our work. We have heard the petitions of Africans and of abolitionists speaking in their behalf. Some here are sympathetic to these pleas for freedom. Others are not. But we have debated this issue at length, and after three months of difficult negotiations, compromises have been reached, decisions made, language drafted and approved. The matter is settled. Neither you nor whatever powers have sent you here can undo what is done."

I was not to be put off so easily. "Sirs," I said, "I have come to tell you that the matter of slavery will not be settled by your compromises. And even when it is ended by armed conflict and domestic turmoil far more devastating than you hope to avoid here, the potential evil of giving priority to property over human rights will remain. Can you not address the contradiction in your words and deeds?" . . .

"Your deliberations here have been secret," I continued, "and yet history has revealed what you here would hide. The Southern delegates have demanded the slavery compromises as their absolute precondition to forming a new government."

"And why should it not be so?" a delegate in the rear called out. "I do not represent the Southern point of view, and yet their rigidity on the slavery issue is wholly natural, stemming as it does from the commitment of their economy to labor-intensive agriculture. We are not surprised by the determined bargaining of the Georgia and South Carolina delegations, nor distressed that our Southern colleagues, in seeking the protection that they have gained, seem untroubled by doubts about the policy and morality of slavery and the slave trade". . .

I shook my head. "Here you are then! Representatives from large and small states, slave states and those that have abolished slavery, all of you are protecting your property interests at the cost of your principles." . . .

"Do you recognize," I asked, "that in order to gain unity among yourselves, your slavery compromises sacrifice freedom for the Africans who live amongst you and work for you? Such sacrifices of the rights of one group of human beings will, unless arrested here, become a difficult-to-break pattern in the nation's politics." . . .

51

"Woman!" a delegate shouted from the rear of the room. "Explain to us how you, a black, have gotten free of your chains and gained the audacity to come here and teach white men anything."

I smiled, recognizing the eternal question. "Audacity," I replied, "is an antidote to your arrogance. Be assured: my knowledge, despite my race, is far greater than yours." ... "I cannot believe," I said, "that even a sincere belief in the superiority of the white race should suffice to condone so blatant a contradiction of your hallowed ideals." ...

The delegate had gotten to his feet, and was walking slowly toward me as he spoke. "This contradiction is not lost on us. Surely we know, even though we are at pains not to mention it, that we have sacrificed the rights of some in the belief that this involuntary forfeiture is necessary to secure the rights of others in a society espousing, as its basic principle, the liberty of all."

... "It grieves me," he continued, "that your presence here confirms my worst fears about the harm done to your people because the Constitution, while claiming to speak in an unequivocal voice, in fact promises freedom to whites and condemns blacks to slavery. But what alternative do we have? Unless we here frame a constitution that can first gain our signatures and then win ratification by the states, we shall soon have no nation. For better or worse, slavery has been the backbone of our economy, the source of much of our wealth. It was condoned in the colonies and recognized in the Articles of Confederation. The majority of the delegates to this convention own slaves and must have that right protected if they and their states are to be included in the new government."

He paused and then asked, more out of frustration than defiance, "What better compromise on this issue can you offer than that which has been fashioned over so many hours of heated debate?"

The room was silent. The delegate, his statement made, his question presented, turned and walked slowly back to his seat. A few from his state touched his hand as he passed. Then all eyes turned to me.

I thanked the delegate for his question and then said, "The processes by which Northern states are even now abolishing slavery are known to you all. What is lacking here is not legislative skill but the courage to recognize the evil of holding blacks in slavery, an evil that would be quickly and universally condemned were the subjects of bondage members of the Caucasian race. You fear that unless the slavery of blacks is recognized and given protection, the nation will not survive. And my message is that the compromises you are making here mean that the nation's survival will always be in doubt. For now in my own day, after two hundred years and despite bloody wars and the earnest efforts of committed people, the racial contradiction you sanction in this document remains and threatens to tear this country apart."

Geneva Crenshaw makes it abundantly clear: Even today, in the late twentieth century, we still feel the reverberations of the compromise struck at the Constitutional Convention 200 years ago. The exclusion of blacks from the document, the nod given to enslavement, the degradation of blacks as less than "whole" human beings—all these factors set the stage for the racial hatred that colors the actions of today's Ku Klux Klan; that erupts into the ugliness of Forsyth County, Georgia, and Howard Beach, New York; that results in the devastating statistics on today's black families. Consider a few of these statistics:

- The leading cause of death among black men under 25 is homicide.
- More black men are in prison than in college.
- Black families have a median income of $19,329, while white families enjoy a median income of $33,915.
- Teens are dropping out of school at a rate that exceeds 50 percent.
- Fifty percent of black families with children under 18 are headed by single women.

Our forebears compromised the future of blacks and generation after generation of black children. Later amendments attempted to remedy the situation, but the die had been cast.

The Evolving Constitution

Our profound hope now is to pick up the spirit of that flawed, altogether human document and carry on. We must use the "We the People" preamble to achieve civil rights gains; we must deploy the equal protection clause to achieve an ever-elusive equality. We must because these are the only weapons we have. What a bitter irony: Blacks now use the Constitution, the very same document that caused them so much woe, as a sword with which to avenge their rights. One wonders what the founding fathers would have thought about that.

On May 6, 1987, Supreme Court Justice Thurgood Marshall gave a speech in which he made these same observations. The Constitution, he noted, was "defective from the start," since its protections extended neither to blacks nor women. Justice Marshall concluded:

In this bicentennial year, we may not all participate in the festivities with flag-waving fervor. Some may more quietly commemorate the suffering, struggle and sacrifice that has triumphed over much of what was wrong with the original document, and observe the anniversary with hopes not realized and promises not fulfilled. I plan to celebrate the Bicentennial of the Constitution as a living document, including the Bill of Rights and the other amendments protecting individual freedoms and human rights.[22]

Justice Marshall was severely castigated by many for his remarks; his detractors complained that he was judging the eighteenth-century founders by twentieth-century standards.

But Justice Marshall is correct: In remembering the founders and the document, we must view the events that transpired in 1787 realistically. Indeed, we must take a critical look, for only by doing so can we come to understand that our Constitution is a living document whose imperfections have been and will continue to be remedied over time.

The compromise over slavery may seem to some whites as a minor imperfection that was supported by prevailing public opinion. However, as a black man and one who has dedicated his life to fighting the evils of racism, I find the compromise appalling. For today we live in a society where the Supreme Court still agonizes over civil rights cases in which race remains a dominant issue.

To dismiss Justice Marshall's remarks by arguing that he has indicted eighteenth-century men by twentieth-century standards misses the point. The wisdom, foresight, and sense of justice exhibited by the founders are questionable according to the Constitution's own standards. In the Preamble to the Constitution, the founders sought to form a more perfect union, establish justice, promote the general welfare, and secure the blessings of liberty. The perpetuation of slavery was at odds with the Constitution's mandate. Thus, as Geneva Crenshaw tried gently to explain to the delegates, the compromise created an inherent contradiction between guaranteeing liberty and justice to all and denying these same basic freedoms to blacks.

The Thirteenth and Fourteenth Amendments abolished slavery; ensured protection of the life, liberty, and property of all persons against deprivations without due process; and guaranteed equal protection under the law. The Fifteenth Amendment provided for the participation of blacks in the political process. These amendments highlight the beauty of our Constitution. It is a living document. It has the flexibility to be adapted to varying situations in a changing world. As a member of the federal judiciary, I feel strongly that the courts have a responsibility to interpret the Constitution according to its dictates of equality and justice.

History has shown that sometimes courts must be true to the Constitution's principles in the face of enormous odds. For example, from 1896 to 1954, the doctrine of "separate but equal" governed the lives of black Americans. Under this principle, minorities could be given separate service or treatment so long as it was equal to that provided for whites. The doctrine was not consistent with the Fourteenth Amendment's directive of equal protection under the law. Congress failed to rectify this injustice, and for more than 50 years the doctrine prevailed. It was not until 1954 that the United States Supreme Court upheld the Constitution and overturned the social travesty of separate but equal.

While some may arrogantly refer to this type of action as "judicial activism," I differ and fervently state that this activity is nothing more than interpreting the Constitution to ensure equality for all. As Justice Marshall has stated, legal principles have played an important role in determining conditions for blacks. While these principles have enslaved and segregated by using the law, they finally have begun to win equality through law. I concur totally with Justice Marshall when he states, "The progress has been dramatic, and it will continue." Yet, in spite of what some white people say, we do not live in a color-blind society.

As we celebrate the 200th anniversary of the United States Constitution, we must remember that we are celebrating a document whose truths have been made self-evident only through constant struggle and the evolution of time. In this pluralistic society that we so proudly hold out as an example to the world, we must acknowledge the views of Justice Marshall, who has developed an intimate knowledge of the Constitution through a distinguished career as the director/counsel of the NAACP Legal Defense and Educational Fund, solicitor general of the United States, and associate justice of the Supreme Court.[23] Indeed, he enjoys an international reputation as a drum major for justice and a foot soldier for the Constitution. His critical view of the Constitution is not an act of disloyalty, but rather an act of reflection and of faith in those qualities that have made it a document that today embraces freedom and human rights. We must acknowledge the fact that the original document and those who wrote it were not perfect. By making this acknowledgement, we will understand that our Constitution can be adapted and that it is now fulfilling its original promise, as stated in its Preamble, to "establish Justice" and "secure the Blessings of Liberty" for us all.

The words of the poet Langston Hughes are ever before us as we carry our struggle into the twenty-first century: "America never was America to me, and yet I swear this oath—America will be!"

We must begin to realize that America's social mores have often trampled on freedom and human rights. The double standard that has been applied to people of color can be documented as far back as Plymouth Rock. We all must be committed to educating the masses that blacks and other people of color are also included in the phrase "We the People." If we who believe in equality for all don't join hands to fulfill the promise, then who will?

Notes

1.   Many of the statutory references in this paper are drawn from the wealth of information in A. Leon Higginbotham, Jr., *In the Matter of Color—Race and the American Legal Process: The Colonial Period* (New York: Oxford University Press, 1978).

2.   John Rolfe to Sir Edwin Sandys, January 1620, as noted in Volume 3 of *The Records of the Virginia Company of London*,

Susan M. Kingsbury (ed.), 4 vols. (Washington: GPO, 1933), pp. 24-25.

3. See William W. Henning, *Statutes at Large of Virginia*, Vol. 4 (Richmond, Va.: Franklin Press, 1819-1820), p. 131; Thomas Cooper and David McCord (eds.), *Statutes at Large of South Carolina*, Vol. 3 (Columbia, S.C.: A.S. Johnston, 1836-41), p. 136; Francois-Xavier Martin (ed.), *Public Acts of the General Assembly of North Carolina* 1715-1803, Vol. 1 (Newbern, N.C.: James Iredell, 1804); Allen D. Chandler (ed.), *Colonial Records of Georgia*, Vol. 18 (Atlanta: Franklin Printing and Publishing Co., 1904), p. 102.

4. A "surety" is one who undertakes to pay money or to do any other act in the event that his or her principal fails therein. Everyone who incurs a liability in person or estate, for the benefit of another, without sharing in the consideration, stands in the position of a "surety," whatever may be the form of his or her obligation.

5. Henning, *Statutes at Large of Virginia*, Vol. 1, p. 226.

6. Henning, *Statutes at Large of Virginia*, Vol. 4, p. 131.

7. Act XXII (1660), as cited in Henning, *Statutes at Large of Virginia*, Vol. 2, p. 26.

8. Henning, *Statutes at Large of Virginia*, Vol. 2, p. 270.

9. Higginbotham, *In the Matter of Color*, p. 38.

10. June Purcell Guild, *Black Laws of Virginia*, reprint ed. (New York: Negro University Press, 1969), p. 45. Also refer to Henning, *Statutes at Large of Virginia*, Vol. 1.

11. Higginbotham, *In the Matter of Color*, p. 148.

12. *Ibid.*, p. 148.

13. George H. Moore, *Notes on the History of Slavery in Massachusetts* (New York: Negro University Press, 1968), p. 191.

14. Higginbotham, *In the Matter of Color*, p. 89. The author cites Francis H. Fox's "Discrimination and Anti-Discrimination in Massachusetts Law," 44 B.U.L.Rev. 30, 37 (1964), which states that "9972 towns vot[ed] against the constitution and only 2083 of the towns vot[ed] for it."

15. Cooper and McCord, *Statutes at Large of South Carolina*, Vol. 3, p. 136.

16. *Dred Scott* v. *Sandford*, 60 U.S. 393, 410 (1856).

17. The then-congresswoman spoke these eloquent words during the impeachment hearings of former President Richard M. Nixon before the Senate Judiciary Committee on July 25, 1974. See Barbara Jordan and Shelby Hearon, *Barbara Jordan: A Self Portrait* (New York: Doubleday and Co., 1979).

18. Article 1, Section 2, Clause 3 (last modification on September 17, 1787) of the U.S. Constitution.

19. Article 1, Section 9, Clause 1 (last modified on September 14, 1787) of the U.S. Constitution. Note that following the close of the Constitutional Convention on September 17, 1787, Delaware was the first state to ratify the Constitution, which it did on December 7, 1787; on May 29, 1790, Rhode Island became the last state to ratify it.

20. Max Farrand (ed.), *The Records of the Federal Convention of 1787*, revised ed., Vol. 1 (New Haven and London: Yale University Press, 1966). For a detailed summary of this debate, see Philip B. Kurland and Ralph Lerner (eds.), *The Founders' Constitution*, Vol. 2 (Chicago and London: University of Chicago Press, 1987), pp. 90-91.

21. Excerpted from Derrick Bell, *And We Are Not Saved: The Elusive Quest for Racial Justice* (New York: Basic Books, Inc., 1987).

22. The Honorable Thurgood Marshall, "The Constitution's Bicentennial: Commemorating the Wrong Document?", 40 Vand. L. Rev. 1337, 1342 (1987). Associate Justice Marshall delivered the speech on May 6, 1987, at the Annual Seminar of the San Francisco Patent and Trademark Association in Maui, Hawaii. For an in-depth critique of his speech, see Raymond T. Diamond, "No Call to Glory: Thurgood Marshall's Thesis on the Intent of a Pro-Slavery Constitution," 42 Vand. L. Rev. 93 (1989).

23. Justice Marshall retired from the bench on June 28, 1991, following a long and industrious career dedicated to upholding the principles of the Constitution in its intended anti-majoritarian and evolutionary form.

The struggles to gain the right to vote by those who were locked out have taken place in court, on the battlefield, within the family, in the streets, in state legislatures, and in Congress.

Voting, Voting Rights, and Political Power in American History

Mary Frances Berry

The history of voting in the United States is the history of barriers erected and erased. The invidious reasons for these barriers became more and more obvious during the struggles to eradicate them. Until recently, suffrage was almost exclusively the right of white men. Blacks, in particular, and women, black and white, were excluded. Native Americans, for the most part, could not vote until well into the twentieth century. Asian Americans were excluded by keeping them in a suspended state of alienage to deny them citizenship and thus the right to vote.

The struggles to gain the right to vote by those who were locked out have taken place in court, on the battlefield, within the family, in the streets, in state legislatures, and in Congress. As a result of these legendary efforts, today, near the close of the twentieth century, blacks, women, language minorities, persons with handicaps, propertyless persons, and even some without traditional homes or residences have the right to vote.[1]

Citizenship and Suffrage in Early America

In the colonial period, the right to vote and the right to hold office belonged exclusively to property holders who had a stake in the community. "No taxation without representation"—the popular cry of the American Revolution—forced a rethinking of the principle of property holding as a basis for the franchise.[2] (Today we note that a similar argument concerning lack of representation does not seem to have the same effect when made in favor of the residents of the District of Columbia.) During and after the American Revolution, some states inserted a taxpayer requirement for property holding in state constitutions.[3]

The United States Constitution of 1787 left the establishment of voting qualifications to the states. State suffrage granted national suffrage as well. Native Americans, however, were explicitly denied citizenship in Article I. They were not taxed and therefore, the argument went, needed no representation. Blacks were three-fifths persons for taxation and representation purposes. And women of all races were simply unqualified.[4]

During the 200 years before the Civil War, slaves could not vote. Free Negroes voted when allowed, but by 1830 their right to vote or hold office was revoked universally. Women did not vote individually; they were supposedly represented by their husbands' votes.[5]

Some blacks had the peculiar idea that serving in the military—whether in the Revolutionary War, the War of 1812, or the Mexican War—made them eligible for political rights. Chief Justice Roger B. Taney scotched that notion in his quaint version of history in the Dred Scott case:

> Why are the African race, born in the state not permitted to share in one of the highest duties of the citizen? ... The Answer is obvious; [a black person] is not, by the institutions and laws of the state, numbered among its people. He forms no part of the sovereignty of the State, and is not, therefore, called upon to uphold and defend it.[6]

Taney wrote this history to defend his belief that blacks were not and never had been citizens.

Universal white manhood suffrage without property or taxpayer restrictions became the national rule by 1850.[7] In the 1840s, among white males who had achieved suffrage, voter participation was high, especially in state and local elections. Political parties were sharply delineated, and the campaigns were exciting and presented real choices. Politics was popular entertainment.[8]

Changes Wrought by the Civil War

The next great expansion of the franchise came with the Civil War. Military necessity led to political rights for black males. On the eve of its final defeat, the Confederacy contemplated emancipation and suffrage for black males in return for their support of the South.[9] In the District of Columbia, Congress granted all male residents, black and white, the right to elect their own government.[10] In the last letter he wrote on the subject before his assassination, Abraham Lincoln suggested that black men in Louisiana, where Union victories brought Reconstruction early, be permitted to vote. He wrote to the governor he had appointed, "I only suggest for your private consideration whether some of the colored people may not be let in as, for instance the very intelligent, and especially those who have fought gallantly in our ranks."[11] And smaller Union strongholds of the South such as Hampton, Virginia, and the South Carolina Sea Islands also tried these "experiments" in black citizenship.[12]

In the last years of the Civil War, Northern free Negroes mobilized more vigorously to press for the right to vote. In conventions and meetings, the petitions and proclamations they issued expressed appeals for suffrage. One of the most eloquent was written by Frederick Douglass in 1864:

> We want the elective franchise in all the states now in the union, and the same in all such states as may come into the union hereafter. . . . The position of that right is the keystone to the arch of human liberty; and without that the whole may at any moment fall to the ground; while with it that liberty may stand forever . . . [13]

Douglass and other black and white leaders believed that the

65

abolition of slavery was only a beginning. They were appalled when the Southern states reconstructed themselves by keeping to the old ways. The "reconstructed" states perpetuated the exclusion of blacks from suffrage and holding office by requiring blacks to make certain kinds of employment contracts or be jailed as vagrants. Yet Southern whites refused to let blacks enforce the contracts, denying them permission on the grounds of race and color alone.

Blacks were pleased with the Freedmen's Bureau bill, which brought them some education and the prospect of land for the freedmen. The Civil Rights Act of 1866 promised that if, on account of race, a black person was refused the right to enforce a contract or to lease, rent, or buy property, he or she could press for his or her rights in federal court. But Douglass and others said, This is not enough—we must also have political rights, the keystone in the arch.[14]

Congress investigated and responded by passing the Military Reconstruction Acts beginning in 1867. Participants in the South's war against the United States were disfranchised, while black males were enfranchised. Most significantly, registration and the elections were supervised directly by federal officials of the Union Army.[15] Black males were elected to local, state, and national office— including two black U.S. senators, Hiram Revels and Blanch K. Bruce, both from Mississippi.

During the conventions at which they joined in writing new state constitutions, blacks made clear their understanding of the franchise. They did not propose continuing the disfranchisement of former rebels. They wanted a politics of inclusion rather than exclusion; and the representatives of some states, such as South Carolina, even considered extending suffrage to women. As the *Charleston Advocate* explained in May 1867, "We ... scorn the idea of the white man's party or the black man's party. ... All should be admitted to equal rights and privileges in church and state whatever may be their race or color. ... We should all live together in peace and harmony ... " These state constitutional conventions in which blacks participated adopted universal male suffrage.[16]

The Ramifications of Reconstruction

Blacks learned many things during Reconstruction. Politics brought rewards of patronage and some decision-making influence and power, but did not bring about economic revolution or the redistribution of wealth. Blacks learned that even black politicians who were elected were not revolutionaries in this regard.[17] Some necessary changes could be achieved through the political process; others could not. Blacks also learned that, once given the opportunity for action, the whites whom they had refused to disfranchise were not as generous as the blacks had been. Whites understood that if they could keep blacks from voting by leveling charges of corruption, duplicity, bloodshed, murder, and riot, they could win back power. They forced blacks out of the political arena with the acquiescence and even approbation of Northern public opinion and party officials. The Thirteenth, Fourteenth, and Fifteenth Amendments and some enforcement acts passed in 1870 and 1871 survived amidst the debris, but Reconstruction was over.[18]

Blacks spoke out against the nefarious deeds of the post-Reconstruction period but to little avail. T. Thomas Fortune minced no words when he wrote in the *New York Globe* in 1883, "We have the ballot without any law to protect us in the enjoyment of it. . . . The Democratic party is a fraud—a narrow-minded, corrupt, bloody, fraud, and the Republican party has grown to be little better." Political participation for blacks became fraught with dangerous consequences. A variety of so-called legal measures such as gerrymandering, poll tax requirements, grandfather clauses, and elaborate election procedures were instituted to disfranchise blacks.

Many of these measures also disfranchised poor white males. Farmers' organizations—in particular the Grange, Alliance, and Populist movements—attempted to form alliances between poor whites and blacks but foundered on the primacy of racial considerations. Politically powerful Democrats forced blacks who worked for them to vote for the white-picked candidate or not at all.

67

In some areas—for instance, North Carolina in 1894—black and white populists temporarily gained control. Soon, however, white Democrats, Republicans, and Populists complained that blacks should be removed from politics altogether. Once more, race triumphed over class.[19]

Black Voting Since the 1890s

The last serious federal effort to protect black voting until the modern civil rights movement was the Lodge Federal Elections Bill of 1890. Although the bill passed in the House, it was abandoned in the Senate by Republicans who wanted Democratic support for high tariff and silver legislation. This was the age of Booker T. Washington. In his Atlanta speech of 1895, Washington announced that economic advancement should come before political rights, and only after these had been achieved should blacks attempt to end legal discrimination. Publicly he did not acknowledge a connection between the three realms. Yet, although he scorned the idea of black political involvement when he addressed audiences across the nation, behind the scenes he was actually paying for lawsuits that challenged segregation and disfranchisement. He was the essence of the politician and power broker. He did, in fact, see connections between economic and political power; but he perceived—accurately, perhaps—that it was impolitic to discuss these issues openly and honestly.[20]

Unlike Washington, successive organizations—the Afro-American League, the Niagara Movement, and, after its founding in 1910, the National Association for the Advancement of Colored People—insisted there were social, political, and economic interconnections that perpetuated black subordination. As T. Thomas Fortune put it in 1905, "In a democracy a citizen without a vote would have every other civil and political right denied him."[21] As a result of the aforementioned organizations' efforts, the twentieth-century history of black political participation includes the successful outlawing of grandfather clauses in the courts in 1915.[22] It also includes disallowing Texas' repeated attempts to use white-only primaries as a method of excluding black voting in the only meaningful part of the electoral process. Since the end of Reconstruction, Democratic Party candidates in Texas practically had been assured of election.[23]

Blacks moved northward in increasing numbers in search of economic opportunity and political rights and what they hoped would be less discrimination. In the North during this period from 1890 to 1920, blacks were allowed to vote. But the boss system in the North forced black voters to compete with better established immigrant groups, and the at-large representation system did not make the road as easy as it might have seemed. Further, the large-scale migration of blacks coincided with the Progressive movement, which advocated the reform of city government. However clean government might have become, it was no longer possible for blacks to gain patronage jobs and political influence through the boss system, as immigrant groups had done.[24]

In the South, until the 1960s, a black person faced what James Weldon Johnson described in 1929 as "[t]he grim determination of the southern politician never to allow him to take part in politics—his education, economic progress and moral fitness, notwithstanding—and the specter of force, violence and murder" should it prove necessary to reinforce the politician's determination. These views were expressed not just by plebeian demagogues like Alabama Senator Thomas Heflin and Senator Cole Blease of South Carolina, but even by aristocratic statesmen such as Senator Carter Glass, who was quoted as saying that "the people of the original thirteen southern states curse and spit upon the Fifteenth Amendment—and have no intention of letting the negro vote." We white Southerners, he said, obey the letter of the law, "but we frankly evade the spirit thereof—and propose to continue doing so. White supremacy is too precious a thing to surrender for the sake of a theoretical justice that would let a brutish African deem himself the equal of white men and women in Dixie."[25]

69

The Women's Suffrage Movement

Since Abigail Adams's admonition to her husband to "Remember the Ladies," women have tried to obtain political recognition. At Seneca Falls in 1848, the Declaration of Sentiments summed up the wrongs of man toward woman. Women, black and white, discovered during Reconstruction that the Thirteenth Amendment did not protect them from "the slavery of sex," nor did the Fourteenth and Fifteenth Amendments secure their right to vote. The Supreme Court told them this in patronizing detail in *Minor* v. *Happersett* (1875).[26]

Civil disobedience, picketing, marching, jail stints, and the acts of courageous people including Carrie Chapman Catt, Alice Paul, Ida Wells Barnett, and Mary Church Terrell—added to the work of the movement's founders, Elizabeth Cady Stanton and Susan B. Anthony—placed the Nineteenth Amendment in the Constitution in 1920. Success came 72 years after Seneca Falls and 133 years after the Constitution was approved in Philadelphia. It was not until the Voting Rights Act of 1965, however, that women of color and language minority women would have their political rights guaranteed in our law.[27]

The Rights of Other Disenfranchised Groups

Despite the fact that persons born in this country are citizens by birth, Native Americans had to wait until the twentieth century to be accorded their political rights. In 1887 the Dawes Act granted citizenship to Indians who would leave their tribes and abandon their "traditional" ways of life. In 1901 Congress granted citizenship to Indians living in Indian territory and, in 1919, to those who served in the military in World War I. And in 1924 any other Indians who had not yet been granted citizenship were given the right to vote and to hold office.[28] Issues of meaningfully expanding the vote to disabled and language minority groups awaited the impact of the modern civil rights movement.

Lessons of the Legacy

What can be learned from this history? Perhaps that people vote and run for office when they believe citizenship means something. And that people are more inclined to vote when there are clear distinctions between candidates and their respective proposals.

The history of a people plays an undeniable role. The history of Afro-Americans shows an assiduous use of political involvement as a tool to gain freedom and other rights. Women, on the other hand, registered and voted in lower numbers than men until the 1940s. Not until the 1984 presidential election when Geraldine Ferraro became the Democratic Party's vice-presidential nominee did women's voting participation exceed the rate for men.[29]

Political participation does engender a certain amount of change and respect. In the South, for example, the legal system was very responsive to blacks after the Civil War, when they commanded voting power. Until women, white and black, could vote, the legal system was more responsive to white males. Then, when women got the vote in 1920, the system was responsive to women's demands—until elected officials discovered that women voted like their male relatives. But by 1984 the gender gap had grown so large that it commanded the attention of politicians.

We must protect the right to vote. But if we want people to vote, we must explain clearly what voting can and cannot do. Disappointment will follow if voters believe the government can do what in reality it cannot. We must also explain to voters that politics is only one way of making change. Protest, litigation, and public relations are essential ingredients in politics. One important task is to make voters understand that appointments to the Supreme Court are determined by who is elected to the presidency and the Senate. This will inspire more people to vote. In doing so, we can further our efforts to enhance our democracy and to expand the franchise.

Notes

1. Fourteenth, Fifteenth, and Nineteenth Amendments to the U.S. Constitution; 42 U.S. Code Sections 1972 (a)-(b), 1973 b(f), 1973 aa-1a (1982); *Katzenback* v. *Morgan*, 384 U.S. 641 (1966), upholding voting rights provisions guaranteeing the right to vote to certain persons educated in Puerto Rican schools despite their lack of English language ability; La. Rev. Stat. Ann., Section 18: 531, 564, 1310, 1321-35 (West 1979 & Supp. 1985) on handicapped access; *City of Phoenix* v. *Kolodiejski*, 399 U.S. 204 (1970); *Cipriano* v. *City of Houma*, 395 U.S. 701 (1969); *Kramer* v. *Union Free School District*, 395 U.S. 521 (1969), concerning approval of voting rights to nonproperty owners; Robert W. Collin, "Voting Rights of the Homeless," *Stetson Law Review* 14 (1985), analyzing litigation to allow homeless persons to vote. For general background information, see M. David Gelfand, "Voting Rights and the Democratic Process: Ongoing Struggles and Continuing Questions," *Urban Lawyer* 17 (1985), p. 333.

2. Suffrage was extended to some free blacks before the Revolution. See Derrick Bell, *Race, Racism and American Law*, 2nd ed. (Boston: Little, Brown and Company, 1980), pp. 127-130. In New Jersey, women held the right to vote until 1806, as noted in Mary Frances Berry, *Why E.R.A. Failed: Politics, Women's Rights and the Amending Process of the Constitution* (Bloomington: University of Indiana Press, 1986), p. 30.

3. Willi Adams, *The First American Constitution's Republican Ideology and the Making of the State Constitutions in the Revolutionary Era* (Chapel Hill: University of North Carolina Press, 1980), pp. 196-217 and pp. 293-311 (appendix).

4. Article I, Section 2, of the U.S. Constitution; *Cherokee Nation* v. *Georgia*, 5 Peters 1 (1831), 211; Mary Frances Berry, *Why E.R.A. Failed*, p. 30.

5. Linda Kerber, *Women of the Republic: Intellect and Ideology in Revolutionary America* (Chapel Hill: Institute of Early American History, University of North Carolina, 1980), pp. 18-34.

6. *Dred Scott* v. *Sandford*, 19 Howard 393 (1857), 242, 415.

7. Leon Litwack, *North of Slavery: The Negro in the Free States 1790-1860* (Chicago: University of Chicago Press, 1961); Mary Frances Berry and John W. Blassingame, *Long Memory: The Black Experience in America* (New York: Oxford University Press, 1982), pp. 142-147; Eleanor Flexner, *Century of Struggle: The Woman's Rights Movement in the United States* (Cambridge: Harvard University Press, 1959), pp. 71-77; 143-145.

8. Arthur M. Schlesinger, Jr., *The Age of Jackson* (Boston: Little, Brown and Company, 1950), pp. 471-490; Glyndon Van Deusen, *The Jacksonian Era, 1828-1848* (New York: Harper and Row, 1959), pp. 1-5.

9. Clarence L. Mohr, *On the Threshold of Freedom: Masters and Slaves in Civil War Georgia* (Athens: University of Georgia Press, 1986), pp. 273-276.

10. James M. McPherson, *The Struggle for Equality: Abolitionists and the Negro in the Civil War and Reconstruction* (Princeton: Princeton University Press, 1964), p. 374.

11. Letter from President Abraham Lincoln to Governor Michael Hahn, March 13, 1864, in Vol. 7 of *The Collected Works of Abraham Lincoln*, Roy P. Basler, ed. (New Brunswick, N.J.:

Rutgers University Press, 1953), p. 243. See also Kenneth Stampp, *The Era of Reconstruction* (New York: Knopf, 1965), pp. 47-48. Stampp notes that while Southern states were enfranchising blacks, Northern states such as Connecticut, Ohio, Michigan, Minnesota, and Kansas considered and rejected black suffrage.

12. Willie Lee Rose, *Rehearsal for Reconstruction: The Port Royal Experiment* (Indianapolis: Bobbs-Merrill, 1964), pp. 335-336 and 389; Robert F. Engs, *Freedom's First Generation: Black Hampton, Virginia* (Philadelphia: University of Pennsylvania Press, 1979), pp. 189-192.

13. Philip Foner, ed., *The Life and Writings of Frederick Douglass*, Vol.3 (New York: International Publishers, 1952), pp. 418-420.

14. *Ibid*, p. 420; Mary Frances Berry, *Military Necessity and Civil Rights Police: Black Citizenship and the Constitution 1861-1868* (Port Washington, NY: Kennikat, 1977), pp. 94-97.

15. 14 U.S. Stat. 428 (1867); XV U.S. Stat. 2 (1867); XV U.S. Stat. 14 (1867); XV U.S. Stat. 41 (1868).

16. John Hope Franklin, *Reconstruction: After the Civil War* (Chicago: University of Chicago Press, 1961), pp. 85-126; Stampp, *The Era of Reconstruction*, pp. 141-142.

17. For example, see Thomas Holt, *Black Over White: Negro Political Leadership in South Carolina during Reconstruction* (Urbana: University of Illinois Press, 1977), pp. 152-170.

18. Michael Perman, *Reunion Without Compromise: The South and Reconstruction, 1865-1866* (Cambridge: Harvard University Press, 1973), pp. 321-336; and Michael Perman, *The Road to*

Redemption: Southern Politics, 1869-1878 (Chapel Hill: University of North Carolina Press, 1984), pp. 17-21.

19. J. Morgan Kousser, *The Shaping of Southern Politics Suffrage Restriction and the Establishment of the One Party South 1880-1910* (New Haven: Yale University Press, 1974), pp. 139-223.

20. Louis Harlan, *Booker T. Washington: The Making of a Black Leader* (New York: Oxford University Press, 1972), pp. 288-303.

21. See *The Colored American Magazine* (December 1905).

22. See *Guinn* v. *United States*, 238 U.S. 347 (1915).

23. In a series of Supreme Court cases, the Court addressed the issue of using white-only primaries to exclude black voting, ultimately outlawing various restrictive attempts in 1953. See *Nixon* v. *Herndon* 273; *Nixon* v. *Condon*; *Grover* v. *Townsend*; *Smith* v. *Allwright*; *Terry* v. *Adams*. See also Darlene Clark Hine, *Black Victory: The Rise and Fall of the White Primary in Texas* (Millwood, NY: KTO Press, 1979).

24. James Q. Wilson, *Negro Politics: The Search for Leadership* (Glencoe, Ill: The Free Press, 1960), pp. 21-47.

25. James Weldon Johnson, "A Negro Looks at Politics," *American Mercury* 18 (September 1929), pp. 88-94. As quoted in Berry and Blassingame, *Long Memory*, pp. 168-169.

26. See 21 Wallace 163 (1875).

27. Berry, *Why E.R.A. Failed*, pp. 30-43, as well as notes cited

therein. See also Rosalyn Terbourg-Penn, "Discrimination Against Afro-American Women in the Woman's Movement, 1830-1920," as quoted in Filomena Steady, ed., *The Black Woman Cross-Culturally* (Cambridge: Schenkman Publishing Co., 1981), pp. 301-316.

28. U.S. Commission on Civil Rights, *Indian Tribes: A Continuing Quest for Survival* (Washington, D.C., 1981), pp. 20-21.

29. Citizens Commission on Civil Rights, *Barriers to Registration and Voting: An Agenda for Reform* (Washington, DC: Citizens' Commission on Civil Rights, 1988).

The Franchise
From Reconstruction
to the Present

I know of no major circumstances involving the evolution of the Constitution that were not embedded in intense political struggle.

The Civil War Amendments: The Second Constitution and The Evolving Political Struggle

Charles V. Hamilton

As a political scientist, I would like to discuss the Civil War Amendments in the context of the political struggle and governmental system in which they were cast. The Constitution of the United States is, after all, a political document. It was brought into being as such, and its perpetuation and modifications over the years, through formal amendments and by interpretation, have been the result of political struggle.

To view the Thirteenth, Fourteenth, and Fifteenth Amendments—the so-called Civil War Amendments—as important additional components of an existing document, and to suggest that those amendments substantially changed the original document and the previous 12 amendments is, I believe, eminently accurate. More than a few observers in recent times have admonished us to be more balanced in our celebratory assessment of the 200-year-old Constitution.

There is no better or more telling observation on this point than that made by Supreme Court Justice Thurgood Marshall. Speaking at the annual seminar of the San Francisco Patent and Trademark Law Association on May 6, 1987, in Maui, Hawaii,

Justice Marshall said:

> I do not believe that the meaning of the Constitution was forever "fixed" at the Philadelphia Convention. . . . Nor do I find the wisdom, foresight and sense of justice exhibited by the Framers particularly profound. To the contrary, the government they devised was defective from the start, requiring several amendments, a civil war and momentous social transformation to attain the system of constitutional government, and its respect for the individual freedoms and human rights we hold as fundamental today. . . . For a sense of the evolving nature of the Constitution we need look no further than the first three words of the document's preamble: "We the People." When the Founding Fathers used this phrase in 1787, they did not have in mind the majority of America's citizens. . . . While the Union survived the civil war, the Constitution did not. In its place arose a new, more promising basis for justice and equality, the 14th Amendment, ensuring protection of the life, liberty, and property of all persons. . . . We will see that the true miracle was not the birth of the Constitution, but its life nurtured through two turbulent centuries of our own making. [emphasis added]

The "Second Constitution," initiated by the Civil War Amendments, in essence built on and provided substantive opportunities to utilize the government structures set forth in the "First Constitution." Those structures remained intact, but now the Civil War Amendments, each in its own way, promised something the Constitution's Framers had denied. These three new amendments freed people, granted them citizenship status, and offered them the initial political wherewithal to function in the polity as potential voters. These amendments invited them in and, indeed, expanded the base of civic participation.

In this sense, the amendments do constitute a second Constitution—or perhaps more precisely, an expanded Constitu-

80

tion—for without them there could be no legitimacy of the political system for millions of people. Yet at the same time, given these amendments in a different governmental structure—one without the checks and balances provided by Congress and the courts—one could question their efficacy. In other words, without the First Constitution in place, the Second Constitution might not be as effective.

The Evolution of the First Constitution

The First Constitution set up structures of governance characterized by separation of powers and a federal state. There would be many checks and balances precisely because the Philadelphia Framers feared that without such restraints, government, composed of inherently ambitious men, would likely become tyrannical. Thus, "ambition must be made to counteract ambition," we are told by Madison in the *Federalist Papers*. Therefore, the three separate branches share powers in various spheres, one branch not being able to operate in some instances without the concurrence of another branch, and even permitting, we were told 14 years later in *Marbury* v. *Madison*, the judiciary to declare acts of the other two branches unconstitutional.

Without question, the First Constitution grew out of a set of ideological orientations that embodied a strong preference for the minimal state, a market economy, and individual liberty (at least for some individuals). The First Constitution was the product of men who fully understood the socioeconomic consequences stemming from the political wrath of a subjected group because they themselves had experienced such consequences. Dan Shays' 1787 rebellion of low-income debtors against tax collectors and property foreclosures in Massachusetts was hardly unknown to them. And neither should we forget how deeply divided Americans were in the 1780s: debtors against creditors, farmers against merchants, advocates of paper money as legal tender against those creditors who saw such currency as essentially worthless. As a result, the document those Framers

81

crafted was very much a product of the politico-economic conditions of those times.

The Emergence of a "Second" Constitution

The Civil War Amendments were no less. Just as a particular political situation, the war, was the catalyst, the continuing political struggle provided the ongoing context. Thus, as Thurgood Marshall noted, the Constitution's "life" has been "nurtured through two turbulent centuries of our own making."

The precise document in 1860 was no more fit to deal with society's problems at that moment in history than the Articles of Confederation had been in the 1780s. Therefore, though the Thirteenth, Fourteenth, and Fifteenth Amendments were enacted, the struggle would continue. The words of the Thirteenth Amendment declaring the end of involuntary servitude had to be given "life." "Equal protection of the laws" of the Fourteenth Amendment had to be given "life." The language of the Fifteenth Amendment—"The right of citizens of the United States to vote shall not be denied or abridged by the United States or by any State on account of race, color, or previous condition of servitude"—had to be given "life." The point is that this language, this creation of a Second Constitution, these words of expansion were part of an ongoing, and reasonably complicated, governmental structure established in Philadelphia 80 years earlier.

This Second Constitution provided additional substantive rights and opportunities. There would still be counter-checking branches of government. There would still be differential levels of power based on economic resources. Even after the First and Second Constitutions were combined, a political struggle still had to be mounted to implement those rights and opportunities. This was precisely what happened.

The Thirteenth Amendment was considered by Congress to need further bolstering against the so-called "black codes" enacted in several states.[1] Thus, the Civil Rights Act of 1866 was passed. But sensing that blacks were still vulnerable, Congress designed the Fourteenth Amendment in part to validate and strengthen the 1866 Act; the amendment was ratified in 1868. The Fifteenth Amendment, which related to the franchise, was ratified in 1870. Congress also promptly passed the 1870 Enforcement Act. Civil rights legislation followed in 1871 and 1875.[2]

The Role of Congress and the Judiciary

A decade of constitutional amendments and congressional legislation ensued. The institutional leader was Congress, not the president, not the courts, not the states. The checks and balances of the First Constitution were called into play. When President Andrew Johnson vetoed the Civil Rights Bill of 1866,[3] Congress overrode that veto. When Southern states, especially Georgia, Alabama, and Mississippi, sought to nullify the Thirteenth Amendment, Congress countered.

Given the nature of the surviving elements in the First Constitution, this political struggle would require mobilization and multiple strategies. When one institutional avenue—perhaps the executive branch or Congress—was effectively closed off, another had to be tried. In fact, what we saw during the next approximately 80 years, from the end of congressional Reconstruction until 1957, was a situation wherein another branch—the judiciary—was turned to as the most receptive to the demands of the beneficiaries of the Second Constitution. But this route really did not begin to prove effective until the "grandfather clause" was overturned in franchise cases brought during the twentieth century. Indeed, no national branch of government was helpful from the dismal years following Reconstruction into the first decades of the new century.

While immigrant groups could come to this country during that period and immediately enter the market economy (albeit, in many instances as cheap and exploited labor) and join the urban political machines, black Americans had to go into courts and argue out the meaning of the Second Constitution. While some groups could gain skills as negotiators of contracts, blacks—functioning under the Second Constitution—had to master the skills of constitutional interpretation. Therefore, the political struggle growing out of the Second Constitution had a distinctive constitutional-rights orientation to it.

Citizenship status for blacks depended in large part on what lawyers and judges said, not so much on what voters in elections could extract from the electoral process. Hence, the Constitution took on added significance for blacks, since no group other than Native Americans in this country has had its day-to-day existence so closely tied to that document as they have. To them it is not some abstract set of principles to be recited on periodic celebratory occasions. And, therefore, its basic weaknesses are all too clear and significant.

This aspect of politicization should not be overlooked. A people so politicized understandably would tend to develop more than a modicum of cynicism when those who have been able to take the Constitution for granted seem to sing its praises too loudly—and, one might add, hypocritically.

Not only were the electoral branches, Congress and the presidency, less available after the end of Reconstruction, thus forcing reliance on the courts, but the Tenth Amendment (the so-called States' Rights Amendment) had to be dealt with because it reserved power to the states. Federalism—another important surviving element of the First Constitution—was still a factor and became the subject of a protracted judicial debate in implementing the Second Constitution.[4]

Neither should we forget that other forms of political action were pursued. There were periodic mass protest actions—for example, against segregated street cars in Atlanta in 1908, and against employment discrimination in the North in the 1930s, when the slogan was "Don't buy where you can't work."

Obviously, breathing life into the Second Constitution was not a struggle with only one strategy. And we certainly know that political action in one sphere frequently served to politicize and motivate action in another sphere.

A Protracted Period of Struggle

The multi-structured surviving features of the First Constitution had advantages as well as disadvantages for the evolving political struggle. Political scientists who call themselves students of American pluralism point to these features as viable aspects of the American constitutional system. The American pluralist system, they suggest, offers several different access points: If the legislature is unresponsive, then turn to the courts or to the executive; if there is no efficacious response, then exercise one's First Amendment right of protest.

What the Civil War Amendments did was to announce that blacks could get into the game. To be sure, the game already had started, and some teams already had had several turns at bat and had scored several runs. To be sure, some players had better equipment. And to be sure, there was always the question of whether the umpires were calling the game fairly, applying the same set of rules to all participants.

For some of us, the Second Constitution certainly spoke to many of these elements of inequality even as it sparked a protracted period of political-constitutional struggle.

Taking the second, expanded Constitution in hand, advocates made powerful arguments on behalf of blacks that private citizens could not discriminate, that racial covenants could not be enforced, that political parties could not devise disingenuous schemes to exclude black citizens from party primaries, that (to quote Judge John J. Parker) "the state or the political party could not do indirectly what the U.S. Constitution and the courts had prohibited them from doing directly."

But it was always clear that salvation did not rest with any one mode of political struggle or with any one governmental institution.

When Congress, the executive branch, and the courts did not respond to civil rights demands, threatened mass protest led to Executive Order 8802 at the beginning of World War II.[5] On more than a few occasions in this struggle, we have seen protest as the catalyst for subsequent action from the formal structures of governance.

The structural features of the First Constitution—namely, a pluralist system providing multiple access points—were combined with the expanded, egalitarian features of the Second Constitution to make the political struggle more legitimate, if not more satisfying. The results would still be incremental and grudging.

As more blacks became voters in places previously closed to them, they could combine a franchise strategy with a litigation strategy and then even add a protest strategy. It is this expanded nature of the Second Constitution that gives greater credibility to what the Framers did in 1787. In many ways they created a structure of governance, but they closed it off to too many.

That structure, however, meant that those who would eventually be brought in—through the nurturing of life that Thurgood Marshall talked about—would need to be able to maximize the opportunities offered by structural diversity. This is so because, while governmental institutions persist, the people who occupy the positions change. Sympathetic occupants today can and do give way to unsympathetic occupants. A court once available to check Southern segregationists might later become the target of a more sympathetic legislative branch that would be required to countermand court rulings. The possibility for that checking and balancing is an important surviving feature of the First Constitution. And a fundamental value of the Second Constitution is that it gave previously enslaved and disfranchised people more tools and a substantive basis to take advantage of the pluralist system.

What the Future Might Hold

Even as we continue to function with the same basic separation of powers and federalist structures that have been in place for the last 200 years, we have seen other innovations not spawned by the Constitution: the development of political parties and of a vast bureaucracy, the emergence of a rapidly changing economy, the growth of an influential national media, and the proliferation of interest groups. All of these phenomena constitute the stuff of an evolving political struggle. If the current Supreme Court proves less amenable to civil rights advocates, efforts must be increased with the other components of the system to countermand the Court.

The persistent struggle for human dignity and political viability in the American constitutional system has never relied only on one approach or on one institutional avenue. This was true at the beginning. It is no less true today. Bill Clinton has called for increased efforts focusing on the National Governors Association and the Conference of State Legislators as an example of the activity of politically diverse strategies.

I know of no major circumstances involving the evolution of the Constitution that were not embedded in intense political struggle. We must not forget the heated political context that brought forth John Marshall's judicial review decision in *Marbury* v. *Madison*. There the outgoing Federalists contended with the incoming Jeffersonian Republicans, jockeying for positions of hegemony, on the heels of the first significant change in regime in the new republic. The losers in the electoral struggle turned to another branch—the courts—to protect their political interests.

And so it has been throughout the history of American constitutional development: a constant shifting back and forth, different branches at different times being called upon to serve as protectors of differing interests. Who knows this better than the intended beneficiaries of the congressionally sponsored Civil War Amendments? And surely those beneficiaries also know they cannot rely on any single structure of the pluralist system to protect their interests in perpetuity.

We may well be at that juncture where a strategic shift in

political effort is required—not because one branch is inherently more efficacious than the others, but because the Second Constitution permitted the increased viability of expanded options. Regimes change, forcing us to adapt to new configurations of political power. The expanded Second Constitution made this scenario more available to more people.

The document the Framers of the Constitution produced was woefully incomplete. They pronounced more than they produced, thereby giving rise to a 200-year-old "American dilemma." Their initial work had to be ameliorated, thus, the creation of the Second Constitution.

One could say that the Civil War Amendments, the subsequent legislative efforts, and the evolving political struggle over the ensuing century made the Philadelphia Framers and their work seem a bit more honest and a lot more civilized.

Notes

1. The so-called "black codes" were state laws that subjugated freed blacks in all former slave states.

2. The civil rights legislation enacted in 1871 and 1875 sought to spell out the protections of the Fourteenth Amendment.

3. President Andrew Johnson vetoed the Civil Rights Bill of 1866 because he was against Congress's approach to post-Civil War Reconstruction.

4. The debate about federalism affected the black population because if the Southern states had power under the Tenth Amendment, they could continue their segregation laws.

5. Executive Order 8802 prohibited employment discrimination in war plants.

Is the job done? Far from it. One thing we have learned is that the right to vote depends on much more than simply being able to register.

Development of the Franchise: 1957-1980

Armand Derfner

Voting rights in America underwent a remarkable transformation between 1957, the year of the first civil rights act since Reconstruction, and 1980, when a peaceful revolution had begun to transform the politics of the South and the Southwest.

The modern civil rights movement was already in full swing by 1957. The integration of the armed forces, *Brown* v. *Board of Education*,[1] the Montgomery bus boycott, the desegregation of Little Rock High School—all of these events had already taken place.

In 1957 Congress finally broke a filibuster to pass the Civil Rights Act of 1957. It was a modest beginning, as it did little beyond authorizing the Justice Department to bring civil suits against voting discrimination. Only a handful of suits were filed, and these didn't get very far.[2] The law was strengthened in 1960 and again in 1964, but it never produced any significant progress in actual registration; because it relied on litigation and simply tried to streamline the judicial process, it was an effort that was bound to fail. J.P. Coleman, then governor of Mississippi (and later, unfortunately, a Fifth Circuit judge), noted that the law would fail because "any legislature can pass a new law faster than a court can strike it down."

Underhanded Tactics Aimed at Blacks

Some of the tactics to prevent voting were, of course, spectacular. It was not just the specific barriers—"literacy tests, poll taxes, and so on"—but the fact that the right to vote was in the hands of local princes and dukes known as registrars and clerks, thereby giving them all the freedom in the world. Each time one tactic was eliminated, another would replace it until Congress could be stirred to act. That was, inevitably, a losing race for black voters.

For example, one of the provisions added to the civil rights law in 1964 said simply that a voter could not be disqualified for making an error that was not material in determining qualifications. This little provision was to deal with situations in which an applicant filling out the registration form would come to "age" and put down, say, "33." At that point the registrar would chuckle, "Sorry, boy, you fail. I can tell from your date of birth that your age is really 33 years, four months, and 16 days."

In one county in southside Virginia, the system was even more refined. Virginia state law said you had to fill out your registration application with no assistance. So the registrar would show the application form to a black applicant and then hand it to him face down. You see, if the applicant got to look at the questions while answering them, that would be assistance, which was barred by state law.[3]

Stopping this kind of nonsense took both an act of Congress and a lawsuit, an indication of how slowly things moved. In fact, as an example of the glacial pace, the Justice Department filed a suit in Dallas County (Selma), Alabama, in 1960, when one percent of that county's blacks of voting age were registered. By 1965, when Dr. King came to Selma, the suit had doubled the number of black registrants all the way to two percent![4]

Civil Rights Laws Between 1957 and 1964

The Civil Rights Acts of 1957, 1960, and 1964 were critically important in several ways. First, the experience of implementing these laws showed how ferocious the resistance to black voting

92

was and how little traditional legislation could accomplish. Second, these laws, modest as they were, stretched the limits of Congress's constitutional power to enforce the Fourteenth and Fifteenth Amendments; as a result, statutes that would have been struck down in the nineteenth century now were being upheld. Third, these laws established that the federal government was committed to securing the franchise, and even if that commitment was halfhearted at the start, the opposition seemed to goad federal officials into stronger action. All these developments were to bear fruit in 1965.

In thinking back to those days, we also have to disregard our modern notion that the Constitution by itself protects the right to vote. For the fact is that the equal protection clause of the Fourteenth Amendment, which we now regard as a basic shield against unfair voting laws, did not exist as far as voting was concerned. The first time the equal protection clause was applied to eliminate a voting restriction was in 1965, when the Supreme Court struck down a Texas law barring servicemen from voting; Texas had argued that the servicemen weren't really residents.[5]

What about redistricting? That didn't exist before 1960 either, because the Supreme Court consistently had held that districting, malapportionment, and gerrymandering were "political questions" beyond the capacity of the courts to deal with. The chink in that armor was the Tuskegee case of 1960. After blacks started registering in Macon County, Alabama, the town fathers simply redrew the boundaries and changed the town of Tuskegee from a square to an "uncouth 28-sided shape" (the Supreme Court's words). Except for four residents, every black person who lived in town was suddenly drawn outside the boundaries. The Supreme Court finally couldn't hold its nose any longer and declared that there comes a point when things have gone too far to be immune from the Constitution.[6]

The Tuskegee case led directly to reapportionment decisions, including the one-person-one-vote rule and the rule, first expressed in the Texas case, that the equal protection clause protects against discriminatory (not just racial) restrictions regarding the right to vote.

The Voting Rights Act of 1965

Thus by the early 1960s we find that Congress was passing voting rights laws; the courts were beginning to grope toward an understanding that there is a right to vote the Constitution must protect; the executive branch was being pulled into the battle; and, perhaps most important, the people of the nation were coming to recognize that a right that people are prepared to die for must be worth something. The freedom rides and all the other events we remember so well made people recognize the depth of the moral issues involved as well as the seriousness of the political issues.

The dramatic culmination of these developments was the Voting Rights Act of 1965, which represented a radical shift away from the earlier approaches. The heart of the act was the banning of literacy tests, as well as the virtual banning of poll taxes. The key to the act, though, was not so much the specifics as the fact that control over the process was taken out of the arbitrary hands of local clerks and registrars. The reality of this change was brought home to them by sending federal examiners to register voters in the most intransigent counties.

The shift in power was further brought home by the preclearance provision of Section 5, which told the counties that they could no longer stay one step ahead of the law but would have to get permission to change their laws. Moreover, it dictated that such permission would not come from hometown courts but from Washington, D.C.[7] The medicine was so strong that it was drafted as temporary legislation scheduled to expire in five years.

The Voting Rights Act charted a new direction for our country and reflected a new understanding of the franchise. It said: We are through; we are not going to tolerate these judicial charades anymore. It also said: The right to vote is a matter of national concern, not a local preserve, and from now on we are going to protect it.

With its strong remedies, shifting so much responsibility from the states to the federal government, a statute like this would have been politically and constitutionally unthinkable 10 years before. If the Voting Rights Act of 1965 had come before the Supreme Court in 1955 or even in 1960, it almost certainly would have been declared unconstitutional; it was the experience of that decade that paved the way for the act. Unlike the 1800s, when efforts to protect the vote foundered on political opposition and judicial obstructionism, now the concept of an inherent right to vote was gaining enough currency to make society and government move to protect it. This would become even clearer in the next few years as attempts were made to turn the clock back.

The Voting Rights Act brought great changes in its first few years. Between 1965 and 1968, millions of blacks registered to vote, and the travesty of heavily black counties with few or no black voters virtually disappeared. The Nixon administration, with its Southern strategy, seized on the act's success to argue that major parts of it (mainly the preclearance provisions of Section 5) should be allowed to expire after the first five-year period. That effort failed; instead of being terminated, the act was strengthened, and the right to vote was expanded.

Elimination of Literacy Tests

Literacy tests, which had been suspended in the Deep South, were not suspended nationwide until the 1970 extension of the Voting Rights Act. It may be hard for us today to recognize the significance of this change in direction. The 1965 act had put an end to such tests in the Deep South, where they were being used overtly to discriminate against black voters.[8] The 1970 extension dealt with 20 more states where literacy tests were used (including New York, Illinois, and California) and where there was no real claim that the tests were being administered discriminatorily.

The nationwide suspension of literacy tests reflected a recognition that illiterate people had just as much right and ability to vote as anyone else. The 1970 extension also gave 18-year-olds the right to vote. When a part of that legislation was deemed unconstitutional, the Twenty-sixth Amendment was quickly passed,

95

putting the 18-year-old's vote beyond question. In addition, in 1975 the Voting Rights Act also reached out to a new category of voters—language minority voters—by providing for language assistance and by bringing them under the coverage of the Section 5 preclearance provisions.

Removal of Other Hindrances to Voting

The courts, meanwhile, were applying the Fourteenth Amendment to strike down other restrictions on the right to vote. Starting with the Texas servicemen's case, the Supreme Court in short order arrived at the doctrine that any restriction on the right to vote is inherently suspect and cannot stand unless it is necessary to promote a compelling interest of the state. Based on this view, the Court struck down property qualifications, long residence requirements, and prohibitions on voting by jail inmates.[9]

With the general elimination of formal barriers to eligibility, people began focusing on other factors that restricted the franchise even for those who were able to register. The focus of Section 5 preclearance shifted away from registration barriers to the more subtle interferences, but the record of constitutional litigation in the courts was more mixed. Early decisions struck down laws restricting candidates' access to the ballot;[10] but as the 1970s wore on, the Supreme Court decisions broke less new ground and in some cases even upheld restrictions such as short registration periods.[11]

On another front, the redistricting cases moved slowly from focusing just on population variances to looking at gerrymandering and vote dilution. Although progress was slower in these cases, there was still a growing awareness that just being registered wouldn't guarantee a full portion of democracy. In 1973, the Supreme Court gave a big boost to dilution challenges when it struck down the use of at-large state legislative elections in Dallas and San Antonio.[12] The standards were difficult but attainable, and a small but growing number of communities eliminated discriminatory at-large elections that had kept black and Hispanic voters shut out of the political process even after large numbers had registered and voted.

During the 1970s there were attempts to stop the clock from moving. In addition to opposing renewal of Section 5 in 1970, the Nixon administration tried to cut back on enforcement of the Voting Rights Act, but it was largely unsuccessful. (Of course, the Watergate scandal probably deserves some of the credit, for it cut short the tenure of two hostile Attorneys General, John Mitchell and Richard Kleindienst, even before President Nixon's departure.) The judges appointed by President Nixon did put some brakes on development of the right to vote, but there was no sign of a real backward movement.

Then in 1980 came two events that were severe tests, threatening to turn the clock radically backwards. The first was the *City of Mobile* v. *Bolden* decision in the spring of 1980, in which a majority of the Supreme Court interpreted the Fourteenth and Fifteenth Amendments as saying that even though a particular pattern, in this case, at-large elections, discriminated in fact against the right to vote on account of race, it would not be struck down unless there was proof that it had been adopted for the purpose of discriminating on account of race.[13] In the Mobile case, the plan had been adopted a hundred years before, and, as the *Birmingham News* later said in an editorial, "It would be quite a trick to subpoena the dead men from their graves to find out what they meant."

The second major threat to the vitality of the right to vote came with the November 1980 election of Ronald Reagan, who made it plain that he planned to turn the clock back and who brought into office a group of people who were deadly serious about fulfilling this mission.

Fortunately, the civil rights coalition addressed these threats during the 1980s, and in 1982 the Voting Rights Act was not only renewed but strengthened. Indeed, one important reason the Voting Rights Act survived during the 1980s was the political power of people enfranchised by the voting rights gains of the 1960s and 1970s.

The Past and Future of Voting Rights

How did the historic gains come about? They were achieved thanks to the tireless work of people in the national civil rights organizations; the courage of countless heroes in Mississippi and other states; the dedication of good-hearted public servants and volunteers; and, very importantly, the determination of those who became enfranchised not to let themselves be pushed backwards.

Is the job done? Far from it. One thing we have learned during this period is that the right to vote depends on much more than simply being able to register. We cannot stop just because it is now possible for disabled people to get to the polls or because it is now possible for a Hispanic voter to cast a vote in a language she can understand or because it is now possible for people to vote in districts that are really fair and not just mathematically equal. Looking back is valuable only if "We the People" are spurred to overcome the challenges we still face.

Notes

1. 347 U.S. 483 (1954).

2. Donald Strong, *Negroes, Ballots and Judges: National Voting Rights Legislation in the Federal Courts* (University of Alabama, University of Alabama Press, 1968).

3. *Wilks* v. *Woodruff*, C.A. No. 4073 (E.D. Va. September 28, 1964).

4. *United States* v. *Dallas County*, 229 F. Supp. 1014 (S.D. Ala. 1964).

5. *Carrington* v. *Rash*, 380 U.S. 89 (1965).

6. *Gomillion* v. *Lightfoot*, 364 U.S. 339 (1960).

7. Section 5 provides that in the covered jurisdictions, new voting practices are unenforceable until they are "precleared" either by the U.S. Attorney General or in a declaratory judgment suit brought by the jurisdiction in the U.S. District Court in the District of Columbia.

8. The states covered by the Voting Rights Act of 1965 were Alabama, Georgia, Louisiana, Mississippi, South Carolina, Virginia, and about half the counties in North Carolina.

9. *Cipriano* v. *City of Houma*, 395 U.S. 701 (1969); *Kramer* v. *Union Free School District*, 395 U.S. 621 (1969); *Dunn* v. *Blumstein*, 405 U.S. 330 (1972); *Goosby* v. *Osser*, 409 U.S. 512 (1973).

10. *Williams* v. *Rhodes*, 393 U.S. 23 (1968).

11. *Marston* v. *Lewis*, 410 U.S. 679 (1973); *Rosario* v. *Rockefeller*, 410 U.S. 752 (1973).

12. *White* v. *Regester*, 412 U.S. 755 (1973).

13. 446 U.S. 55 (1980).

Our resources are so consumed by the initial issue of access to the ballot box and to the swearing-in, we may be ignoring the formidable challenge of ensuring access to the governing and policy-making coalition.

Development of the Franchise: 1982 Voting Rights Amendments

*by Lani Guinier**

One of the most formidable tasks faced by the civil rights coalition was the extension and possible amendment of the Voting Rights Act following Ronald Reagan's election in 1980 and following the Supreme Court decision during the same year in *City of Mobile* v. *Bolden*.[1] That effort highlights the maturation of the civil rights lobby, and it would not have been possible without the successful enforcement of the very act that we were challenged to extend.

A Coalition of Lobbyists and Litigators

In 1980 the civil rights lobby—or, as some of our opponents like to call us, the "civil rights industry"—was a coalition with two very important components that joined together in what became a

---

* This paper essentially represents a transcription of oral remarks delivered to the 1988 Bicentennial Program of the Leadership Conference Education Fund. Despite the use of endnotes, the speech has not been edited either to reflect fully the evolution of my thinking in the intervening years or to transform into a scholarly treatment an informal address by a voting rights advocate. At the time, I was a staff attorney with the NAACP Legal Defense Fund, Inc., and head of its voting rights project.

For a more comprehensive discussion of my views, see Lani Guinier, "The Triumph of Tokenism: The Voting Rights Act and the Theory of Black Electoral Success," 89 Mich. L. Rev. 1077 (1991) and "No Two Seats: The Elusive Quest for Political Equality," 77 Va. L. Rev. 1413 (1991).—*L.G.*

dynamic and intense struggle.[2] There was a creative tension between those of us living inside the Washington Beltway, who suffer from a lot of perhaps unfortunate stereotyping as "chronic compromisers," and those of us from outside the Beltway, who suffer equally from some unfortunate stereotyping as radical, rigid ideologues. These groups joined together with an important mission: to ensure that the promise of the Constitution would be realized for all Americans.

Remember, Ronald Reagan had just been elected. Not only was he elected, but he brought with him a Republican Senate. Not only did he bring a Republican Senate, but the two key members of the United States Senate who would be considering the Voting Rights Act Extension were more than Republicans; they were conservative Republicans. In fact they were not merely conservative Republicans; they were rigidly conservative. I am speaking, of course, about Strom Thurmond, who was chairman of the Judiciary Committee; and Orrin Hatch, who was chairman of the Subcommittee on the Constitution.

Yet the civil rights coalition met in 1981, and with a lot of guts—perhaps a lot more guts than brains at the time—we decided to go for broke: We were going to extend the Voting Rights Act's temporary provisions first enacted in 1965 and due to expire in August 1982. We were going to overturn the Supreme Court decision in *City of Mobile* v. *Bolden* requiring proof of discriminatory purpose in the adoption or maintenance of an election system. We were going to reestablish a results test in the Voting Rights Act.[3] And as if all that weren't enough, we were going to join with our Latino allies to extend the bilingual assistance provision.[4] We put all these priorities together in an omnibus bill within six months after Ronald Reagan had been elected. At the time many people simply thought we were crazy!

We came to Washington with a full plate. We were trying to restore the results test to the Voting Rights Act's Section 2, which prohibited changes in state and local election procedures that would result in the election of fewer blacks and other minorities. Because of the creative tension between the lobbyists and the litigators, we were very careful in our choice of words. The litigators urged that whatever statutory language was adopted be explicit—that it be very straightforward because we would have to take this statute back and enforce it in front of very hostile—or, if not hostile, at least skeptical—members of the federal judiciary. On the other hand, the lobbyists knew that to get anything through Congress, one has to draft legislation using the murkiest language possible in order to bury all conceivable differences lurking behind the ostensible consensus. Employing the term "results," for example, reflected the tension between the litigators looking for explicit language and the lobbyists seeking artful ambiguity.

The Push Toward Legislation

The term "discriminatory effect" had become a lightening rod for opponents to civil rights initiatives in employment and housing. And, indeed, the "effects" language in the Fair Housing Amendment had just been defeated in the last year of the Carter presidency under the organized opposition of Orrin Hatch. Moreover, this same language had been used in another portion of the Voting Rights Act and had come to have a particular, fairly limited meaning. It had been used simply to refer to retrogression—that is, whether blacks were worse off after than they'd been before a particular law was changed, not whether the law was in fact discriminatory in its operation. So while our friends were still in control of the House of Representatives,[5] we introduced this results test and helped coordinate three months of hearings in May, June, and July 1981.[6]

Again there was the creative tension between those inside and outside the Beltway. The insiders were very aware of the legislative timetable necessary to get this bill on President Reagan's desk before August 1982—a critical deadline because that was when the special administrative preclearance provisions would expire.[7] There was also the threat that Reagan was going to veto the bill, so the lobbyists needed enough time before August 1982 for a veto override. There was also the threat that Orrin Hatch, who had so successfully filibustered the Fair Housing Act, would attempt to organize a filibuster of the Voting Rights Act Amendment and its extension. So the lobbyists sought a bipartisan consensus to get the bill passed quickly by an overwhelming majority of the House in the hope that its passage would begin to assume an aura of inevitability. The litigators, on the other hand, wanted to make sure the record was there to support whatever Congress was about to do. Hence, after the filibuster, the veto, and the veto override—when the bill is challenged on constitutional or other grounds—the litigators' primary concern was that the record would exist to support the Voting Rights Act Amendment and extension.

An Unexpected Ally in Congress

The litigators and the grassroots organizers put together an impressive array of hearings to demonstrate that there was a continued and compelling need for the Voting Rights Act in 1981.[8] The litigators, with support from one lay witness after another, made the record for amending and extending the act.[9] In fact, after the hearing in Montgomery, Alabama, we saw a remarkable conversion when one of the primary opponents of the extension at that time, Republican Representative Henry Hyde of Illinois, became outraged about the conditions some of the witnesses described.[10]

Representative Hyde heard witnesses talk about "open-house voting" requiring that—even then, in 1980—blacks had to cast their ballots under the watchful eye of white election officials. He heard about registration hours in Alabama: open at 9 a.m., closed at 4 p.m.[11] He heard about registration places in Virginia that didn't have regular office hours; they were only required to open once a week, and the registrars did not even have to advertise where they were located. Some registration offices in Virginia were set up in the back office of the sporting goods store. He heard testimony that in Mississippi it was easier to get a gun or fishing license than to register to vote.

At the Montgomery hearing, Representative Hyde concluded that the key administrative preclearance provision of the Act, Section 5, must be extended. Hyde's conversion to continuing Section 5 preclearance presented the Leadership Conference on Civil Rights with a fundamental test. He gave us what many saw as the best opportunity for a broad bipartisan consensus with an overwhelming House majority. Because he was prepared to come on board to support the extension of the Voting Rights Act, some Leadership Conference members were prepared to compromise on other provisions in order to obtain Hyde as a cosponsor. Yet many of us saw risks in any new convert to the cause assuming a leadership role so quickly. And it was this process, created by the tension between converting Hyde and maintaining a consensus—not only within the Congress, but within the Leadership Conference—that enabled the Conference to resist a premature compromise.

Even without Hyde's support, on October 5, 1981, H.R. 3112 passed the full House by the overwhelming margin of 389 to 24. We were helped not only by the maturation of the civil rights lobby, not only by the creative tension between the litigators and lobbyists, but by the fact that the Reagan administration was very busy studying this act that the federal government had been enforcing for 17 years.

The administration had not yet taken a position on extension of the Voting Rights Act. It wasn't until a few days before the matter came up in front of the full House that Attorney General William French Smith presented his study to the White House, but by then it was too late.

The Dole Compromise

When we got over to the Senate, our opponents were unnerved by that large House vote, and we were able to get 61 Senate cosponsors on the House bill even before Orrin Hatch had the first hearing in the Senate Subcommittee. Hatch, however, was successful in raising the issue of proportional representation and scaring the living daylights out of the Senate cosponsors as well as members of the Leadership Conference. We were forced to expend considerable energies to disprove any claim that we wanted proportional representation (meaning electoral quotas). So the Senate bill ultimately included the so-called "Dole compromise," proposed by Senator Robert Dole of Kansas, to make that disclaimer explicit: Nothing in the bill was to establish a right based solely on the absence of proportional representation.[12]

But to Hatch's consternation, the Dole compromise proved to be another artful ambiguity. Indeed, many people consider that the Dole compromise was no compromise at all.[13]

The Dole compromise was the codification through statutory language of the 1973 Supreme Court decision in *White* v. *Regester* that said black plaintiffs can successfully challenge a discriminatory election law when they can show that, as a result of the operation of that law in their community, they have less opportunity than whites to nominate or elect representatives of their choice.[14] What began as a compromise, however, proved to be one of the great treasures of the Voting Rights Act.

Because we had to pull in some of the wording from *White*, what Congress ultimately passed was a law that said that minorities have the right to elect representatives of their choice. That was the compromise. So although we thought we were giving minorities the right to register, the right to vote, the right not to be governed by election structures with discriminatory results, the right to assistance where it was needed, and the continued federal presence of the Section 5 preclearance provision, what we got along with all of that was one of the strongest possible statutory statements—a national mandate for group representation.

Congress thereby declared that equal opportunity does not simply mean people of color can go into the voting booth and cast a ballot; it means they have the same opportunity as whites to go into the voting booth and determine who should represent them, the opportunity that their ballot can elect a representative of their choice.

New Challenges for the Civil Rights Coalition

There are a number of issues that have emerged as a result of this acknowledgment of group representation and the 1982 Congressional mandate that minorities have the right not only to vote, not only to cast a ballot, but the right to elect.[15] Some people have questioned whether the right to elect a representative of one's choice is enough. Indeed, if a black person is elected by a majority black constituency as a result of creating a black single-member district, aren't we just reconfiguring the problem? Aren't we moving the polarization from the electorate, whose bloc voting forced us to challenge the dilutive election scheme in the first place, to bloc voting in the legislative halls? Aren't we simply creating some black tokens who will take a seat in the legislature but then be out voted by the white majority when it comes to significant pieces of legislation?

If our goal is to elect minority representatives, how do we keep those representatives electorally accountable? If we are challenging election systems in order to elect representatives, are we also monitoring the performance of those representatives once they are in office? Have we focused exclusively on the electoral process without any sustained exploration of the governance process?

The complex task of policy analysis and legislative decision making—a task with which the Leadership Conference is so familiar at the national level—may be eluding our state and local enforcement efforts. Electoral accountability, not just electability, is critical to preserving the fundamental nature of the rights protected by the Voting Rights Act. The right to vote is crucial not just as a symbol of democratic participation but because it is preservative of all other rights. Yet, because our resources are so consumed by the initial issue of access to the ballot box and to the swearing-in, we may be ignoring the formidable challenge of ensuring access to the governing and policy-making coalition.

107

Finally—and this is an ongoing challenge for the civil rights coalition—haven't we come full circle? We have been very preoccupied with this notion of vote dilution and electoral representation; in the process, haven't we overlooked the fact that the fundamental right to register is still not universally acknowledged? Our federal, state, and local governments still believe that voter registration long before election day is an appropriate test of citizen initiative: a test of the initiative of the individual voter but not of the individual registrar. The registrar, in other words, has no obligation to ensure that everyone eligible is in fact registered and able to participate in elections. Instead, it is the responsibility of the individual voter to find that registration office in Virginia, hidden in the back of the sporting goods store. Only recently has the law in Virginia changed to require registrars to put their names, phone numbers, and addresses in the phone book.[16]

Returning the task of registration to the government will free many volunteers and voter registration groups to engage in that critical process of voter education and turnout, not just on election day but throughout the legislative calendar. There is now pending federal legislation—Senate Bill S. 2061, sponsored by Senator Alan Cranston of California in the Senate and by Representative John Conyers of Michigan in the House—that would create national, uniform voter registration standards and would permit simple, automatic registration procedures.[17] As we endeavor to pass this voter registration bill setting national standards for voter registration, the civil rights coalition will have yet another opportunity to test that creative tension that worked so well in 1982.

Notes

1. In *City of Mobile* v. *Bolden*, 446 U.S. 55 (1980), the Supreme Court ruled that direct proof of racially discriminatory intent is necessary in vote dilution cases. The Court held that the

equal protection clause of the 14th Amendment was not violated if a particular voting practice (in this case at-large elections of city commissioners) simply resulted in voting discrimination.

2. The "civil rights lobby" refers to the Leadership Conference on Civil Rights (LCCR), which is a coalition of 185 national organizations. LCCR serves as the coordinating mechanism for passage of civil rights legislation. Among the principal organizations that lobbied to extend the Voting Rights Act were the NAACP Legal Defense Fund, of which the author was a staff member; the NAACP; the Lawyers Committee for Civil Rights Under the Law; the ACLU; the League of Women Voters; and the Mexican-American Legal Defense Fund (MALDEF).

3. A "results test" establishes that local election practices can be adjudged discriminatory if the results of such practices adversely affect minority voters, even if there was no intent to discriminate when the practice was put into place. Thus, one need only prove a discriminatory effect rather than an intent to discriminate.

4. The principal Hispanic organizations involved were the Mexican American Legal Defense Fund, the National Council of La Raza, and LULAC.

5. Friends of the civil rights legislation included Representative Don Edwards of California, chair of the House Judiciary Subcommittee on Civil and Constitutional Rights; Representative Peter Rodino of New Jersey, chair of the Judiciary Committee; and the House Democratic leadership.

6. These hearings took place before the House Judiciary Committee's Subcommittee on Civil and Constitutional Rights (97th Congress, second session; 18 days in May, June, and July 1991; Serial No. 24, Parts 1, 2, 3).

7. Section 5 of the Voting Rights Act requires that 9 states and portions of 13 other states with a history of racial discrimination in voting submit any changes in "voting qualification or prerequisite to voting, or standard, practice, or procedure with respect to voting" for preclearance by the Department of Justice or the federal courts.

This is a very important component of the Voting Rights Act, since it prevents states from establishing discriminatory practices that might have stayed in place for years while they were being challenged in court. Because of Section 5, such unsavory practices cannot go into effect until after a state receives clearance from either the Justice Department or the federal courts. Thus, the task in 1982 was to extend the Voting Rights Act about to expire in August of that year and to amend it to establish a results test.

8. Hearings before the House Subcommittee on Civil and Constitutional Rights (see note 6).

9. See testimony of Maggie Bozeman of Aliceville, Alabama; Sheriff Prince Arnold of Camden, Alabama; W.C. Patton, former national director of the NAACP Voter Education Project; and Dr. Joe Reed, chairman of the Alabama Democratic Conference. (See note 6, pages 1525 to 1591.)

10. On June 12, 1981, the Subcommittee on Civil and Constitutional Rights met at 9 a.m. in the U.S. Courthouse in Montgomery, Alabama.

11. Limiting office hours impedes people's ability to register. Said Representative Henry Hyde during the Subcommittee proceedings: "I want to say that I have listened with great interest and concern, and I will tell you, registration hours from 9 to 4 is outrageous. It is absolutely designed to keep people who are working and who have difficulty in traveling from registering."

110

12. On June 18, 1982, the Senate overwhelmingly passed the Voting Rights Act extension (S. 1992) by a vote of 85 to 8, rejecting 15 weakening amendments.

13. Senator Dole was the Senate Republican leader and was considered a moderate. Although a member of the Senate Judiciary Committee, up to this point he had remained uncommitted. The language of the so-called Dole compromise preserved the results test and made it clearer than the House version that Congress was not requiring a finding of a violation based on the absence of proportional representation. It used the language of Supreme Court decisions to outline the results test. This allowed senators who supported voting rights to vote for a results test because it seemed to allay their fear that the bill would result in massive federal supervision of all the jurisdictions nationwide in which blacks and other minorities were not proportionately represented.

14. *White* v. *Regester*, 412 U.S. 755 (1973).

15. The 1982 amendments to the Voting Rights Act declared that plaintiffs can establish a violation by showing "that the challenged system or practice, in the context of all the circumstances in the jurisdiction in question, results in minorities being denied equal access to the political process. . . . Section 2 protects the right of minority voters to be free from election practices, procedures or methods, that deny them the same opportunity to participate in the political process as other citizens enjoy. If, as a result of the challenged practice or structure, plaintiffs do not have an equal opportunity to participate in the political processes and to elect candidates of their choice, there is a violation of this section." Report of the Committee on the Judiciary, U.S. Senate, on S. 1992, Voting Rights Act extension, No. 97-417, May 25, 1982, pages 27 and 28.

16. Code of Virginia, Sec. 24.1-43. This change in Virginia law, which occurred in the mid-1980s, provoked heated debate in the state legislature.

17. S. 2061 died in the Senate. Although national voter registration legislation passed the House on February 6, 1990, action was not taken in the Senate.

On June 16, 1992, the House, by a vote of 268 to 153, passed the Motor Voter Registration Bill. The Senate passed the bill on May 20, 1992, by a vote of 61 to 38. The bill, which was vetoed by President Bush on July 2, would have allowed people to register when they apply for or renew their driver's license as well as when they apply for public services such as welfare and unemployment compensation or marriage licenses or hunting permits. Twenty-seven states already have in place a system of motor voter registration.

The Impact of the Vote

*I found that black political power
has had two economic benefits: Black officials
have been able to direct some public sector jobs
toward blacks, and in some communities
there has been a marked increase in
minority contracting.*

Southern Odyssey: Two Decades of Racial Evolution

Margaret Edds

On a warm August day in 1965, Lyndon Johnson sat in the gilded splendor of the President's Room at the U.S. Capitol and, using 100 souvenir pens, signed into law the Voting Rights Act. As the senior statesmen of Congress and the civil rights movement stood by, Johnson proclaimed: "Today, we strike away the last major shackle of fierce and ancient bonds. . . . Today, the American story and the Negro story fuse and blend."

Stunned by the violence at Selma, Alabama, only five months earlier,[1] the nation had acted swiftly to right its shameful record of discrimination in the voting booth. There would be no stopping black Americans now, Johnson vowed. The world was theirs. Godspeed. All this was to flow from the simplest, the least costly, the most basic of American rights, the privilege Johnson had just delivered into the hands of Southern blacks—the right to vote.

Twenty years later, in 1985, I set out to explore the results of two decades of racial evolution under that act. My goal was to assess the degree to which blacks had become part of the South's political power structure, as well as to determine the economic and social impact of blacks' changing status on what long had been the nation's most segregated region. Had Lyndon Johnson's euphoric promise of equal voting rights been achieved? In terms of how people live, had the right to vote mattered?

115

Diverse Black Experiences in the South

With assistance from an Alicia Patterson Foundation fellowship, I took a leave of absence from my job as a reporter for the *Virginian-Pilot/Ledger-Star* newspapers and began focusing on the seven Southern states first covered by the Voting Rights Act: Virginia, North Carolina, South Carolina, Georgia, Alabama, Mississippi, and Louisiana. Over the next several months I visited north Atlanta mansions and Mississippi Delta shanties, big city mayors' offices and dusty country stores, college campuses and civic league meetings. In several hundred interviews the question was the same: Has the South, once smothered and defined by racial prejudice, overcome?

What I found was a region at once vastly changed and much the same. In numbers of elected officials, ease of registration, disappearance of violence, and integration of work places and public facilities, the South of 1985 would have been unrecognizable in 1965. Yet in terms of schools, residential housing, and social patterns, life for many is almost as segregated today as 20 years ago. I saw few schools, fewer restaurants, and still fewer churches where blacks and whites mingled in anything approaching equal numbers. In 1985 there were 38 counties in the South where the majority of the population was black and there was not a single black county commissioner, or only one.[2] The Justice Department was still rejecting election changes it believed were discriminatory. And blacks still trailed badly according to virtually every economic measure; at times, it seemed, those counties run by blacks had had the most economic difficulty of all.

What I did not find in the South was an overarching black political experience. For instance, events in Charlotte, North Carolina, a majority-white city that elected a black mayor in 1983 and 1985, contrasted with those in Richmond, Virginia, where black ascension to power in 1977 was marked by lawsuits, public bickering, and dozens of votes that split along racial lines.

In 1985, state senator Doug Wilder—a black man—was elected lieutenant governor of Virginia, winning 44 percent of the white

116

vote against a clean-cut and inoffensive white opponent.[3] Yet in Sunflower County, Mississippi, birthplace in the 1950s of the white Citizens Council and one-time home to both civil rights heroine Fannie Lou Hamer and former segregationist senator James O. Eastland, past and present collided. Blacks were a majority of the county's population, but in 1985 there was only one black elected official—a school board member—in all of county government. The five county supervisors, the sheriff, the circuit court clerk, the chancery clerk, the tax assessor, the coroner, the two justice court judges, the five constables, the five election commissioners, and four of the five elected members of the school board were white.

In Atlanta I found young black men and women moving steadily into middle- and upper-class jobs. But in Lowndes County, Alabama, a county run by blacks, economic disparity between blacks and whites remained as great as when the Black Panther party was founded there in the 1960s. Six of every ten local blacks lived below the poverty line in 1980, making it the nation's poorest county.[4] Even Atlanta—considered the mecca of black Southerners—mixed failure with success. Six percent of the city's black households had incomes of more than $35,000 in 1980, but a dispiriting 25 percent existed on less than $5,000.

In Edgefield County, South Carolina, home of Senator Strom Thurmond, blacks were euphoric when they assumed political power for the first time in 1985. The election of three black county council members ended a decade-long court battle, and it gave the county's black residents—half of the general population—their first heady taste of political power. But in Greene County, Alabama, there was a disheartening sense that 15 years of majority black rule had not eliminated—or even reduced—many problems. Indeed, a group of blacks—convinced that the county was not being well run—had just joined with white voters to oust some longtime civil rights leaders, an act that would have seemed treasonous a few years earlier.

117

Local Governments Still Controlled by Whites

In 1965, when the Voting Rights Act was passed, there were 300 black elected officials in the nation. By 1985 there were more than 2,300 in the seven states first covered by the act.[5] Black mayors served in Atlanta, New Orleans, Birmingham, and dozens of small cities. Yet in those same Southern states, blacks were 26 percent of the population and, even by the most optimistic projections, held no more than 8 to 10 percent of the elective offices.[6] Most of the offices they did hold were lower level county and municipal jobs. Doug Wilder was unquestionably an anomaly. In the seven states I studied during 1985, blacks equaled or outnumbered whites in 82 counties; in 61 of those counties, whites still ran local government.[7]

A telling example of white insensitivity arose in early 1985 in Dallas County, Alabama, a locale the Selma-to-Montgomery marchers passed through in 1965. That county was 55 percent black, but in 1985 no black person had held county office since Reconstruction. In late 1984, a young black woman—Jackie Walker—was elected tax collector and was to have taken office in 1985. Walker was killed in an automobile crash, however, and the selection of her replacement was left to the all-white county commission. Local blacks argued that Walker's election was a breakthrough for all local black citizens and that someone black should be named to replace her. Despite the vigorous campaign mounted by blacks, the commission voted four to one in favor of appointing to the post the white man whom Walker had defeated.

Election Laws and Dilution of the Black Vote

In terms of voting, I found that literacy tests, violence, and the sort of overt economic pressure that kept blacks away from the polls in 1965 are mostly gone. In the seven states I visited, 31 percent of eligible blacks were registered in 1965.[8] By the mid-1980s, that figure had jumped to 66 percent.[9] In 1965 Mississippi trailed the nation with an abysmal 7 percent black registration;[10] in 1985 it was the second highest in the nation with 86 percent.[11] In Louisiana,

118

Mississippi, and South Carolina, a higher percentage of eligible blacks than whites was registered in 1985.[12] The gap between black and white voting also had narrowed dramatically.

Yet that increase has not occurred without a great and ongoing struggle. Annexations, at-large voting, gerrymandering, and a variety of other devices have been used to dilute black votes. Between 1965 and 1985, the Justice Department blocked more than 1,000 election law changes that it viewed as discriminatory in the seven states. The objectionable changes most often did not directly hamper the ability of blacks to cast a ballot; instead, they diluted the importance of those black ballots cast.

A classic case evolved in Richmond after a 1969 annexation negotiated largely in secret by white officials produced a large pool of new voters, most of whom were white. Overnight an emerging black majority was returned to minority status. The Justice Department objected. The eventual settlement allowed the annexation but only if a ward plan replaced citywide, at-large council elections. In 1977, under the new ward plan, the city installed its first black mayor and council majority. Had the annexation gone forward unchallenged and the system of at-large elections remained intact, there was no reason to expect that the Richmond council would have progressed beyond its tradition of token black representation. The annexation would not have stopped blacks from voting, but, by increasing the pool of white voters, it would have been an equally effective way of ensuring that the black ballots did not count.

Numerous other techniques had a similar result—diluting the impact of black votes. As late as 1985, the Justice Department filed 99 objections to election law changes that it viewed as discriminatory in South Carolina, 30 in North Carolina, six in Mississippi, four in Georgia, and three in Alabama.

In another vein, I found that physical intimidation of black men and women has mostly disappeared, despite isolated incidents like the highly publicized violence in Forsyth County, Georgia, in the

119

winter of 1987.[13] The Ku Klux Klan, though alive, is a shadow of its former self. With rare exception, hooded terrorists and burning crosses are the stuff of history.

If violence had abated by 1985, however, some Southern blacks argued that political and economic intimidation still thrived. Relations between blacks and the Reagan administration—already tenuous—plummeted in the spring of 1985 as federal prosecutors from the U.S. Department of Justice launched a full-scale investigation of alleged voting fraud in the Alabama Black Belt. Among those indicted were several stalwarts of the 1960s civil rights movement.[14] Their supporters—who claimed similar allegations against white politicians had been ignored in the past—said the probe was a Republican attempt to intimidate black voters and sway the 1986 elections. Federal prosecutors noted that several of those who brought complaints were black, and said the motive for prosecution was to protect some poor and uneducated black citizens who were being exploited by the defendants.

The results, however, were not a feather in the administration's cap. Not until the seventh trial was one defendant convicted in October 1985 on four counts of voter fraud. That conviction was eventually overturned, partially because it was imposed by an all-white jury.

Equally murky and unsettling were persistent reports of subtle economic intimidation against black voters, particularly in sections of the Mississippi Delta and rural Georgia. In 1985 and earlier there were numerous accounts, sometimes in court, of plants that "happened" to close late on election day, and of landowners who increased their election-day hires, only to keep those workers in the fields until after the polls had closed. White landowners and entrepreneurs adamantly denied the allegations. But whether by design or accident, some blacks clearly found it difficult to get to the polls due to work conditions. In settings with such a repressive history, the very perception that whites at times conspired to prevent voting no doubt had a chilling effect on black participation.

Segregation Lessening but Not Eradicated

Twenty years after Selma, social interaction between Southern blacks and whites reflected revolutionary progress. The Whites Only signs had become museum relics. In stores and offices across the South, blacks and whites shopped and worked side by side. No black child could be denied a public education equal to that afforded whites. In Selma the street outside Brown Chapel, where marchers gathered in 1965, had been renamed in honor of Martin Luther King, Jr. In Charleston, South Carolina, a portrait of Denmark Vesey, the leader of an aborted nineteenth-century slave revolt in that city, had been hung in the civic center. In Athens, Georgia, at the state university where troopers once accompanied black students to class, Heisman Trophy winner Herschel Walker was a campus hero in the early 1980s. In Birmingham, where police brutality was once legendary and there was not a single police officer in 1965, about three dozen blacks were on the force.

Across the South, however, away from the workplaces and shopping centers, life for many remained almost as segregated in 1985 as in 1965. One could drive the streets of almost any Southern town and stumble upon an invisible line dividing white and black residential sections. Private white academies, created in the wake of school desegregation, flourished. Everywhere, segregated private clubs remained. That was as true at the Piedmont Driving Club, one of Atlanta's most prestigious, as at American Legion posts and Elks Club lodges in dozens of small towns.

In traveling through the South, I wanted not only to evaluate the extent of black political success but also to ask whether electing black officials improves the lives of their black constituents beyond obvious psychological benefits. I found that black political power has had two economic benefits: Black officials have been able to direct some public sector jobs toward blacks, and some communities have had a marked increase in minority contracting. In Richmond, for example, blacks in 1985 held 12 of the city's 30 highest ranking city jobs, versus four in 1977 when a black council majority was

121

elected. City contracts that went to minority firms in Atlanta grew from $41,000 in 1973, when Maynard Jackson became the city's first black mayor, to $27.9 million in 1985.[15]

Black officials have not been able, however, to eliminate severe economic disparities between blacks and whites. Of the seven states' 82 counties with a population at least half black, every single one had a higher level of poverty than its state's average. In all but two of the counties—Madison County, Mississippi, and Orleans Parish, Louisiana—there were fewer high school graduates than in the average county statewide. All but 14 had a higher unemployment rate than average.[16] Worse, those counties where blacks had achieved political control tended to rank at the lowest end of the economic scale.

The difficulty for black officials is underscored by their experience in Macon County, Alabama. That county is the home of Booker T. Washington's Tuskegee Institute, and it has the highest percentage of black residents of any county in the South—86 percent. Over the last decade, officials like Johnny Ford, the mayor of Tuskegee, and Ronald Green, chairman of the Macon County commissioners, have wooed dozens of industries in an attempt to bring them to Macon.

The attractions include a population that is unusually well educated for the rural South, proximity to Montgomery, and the expenditure of hundreds of thousands of federal dollars to provide water and sewer lines, an airport landing strip, and other facilities needed by industry. When I visited Tuskegee in 1985, only two tiny firms—both black owned—had set up shop. By 1986 one of those had closed. The conclusion that Macon County's large black population was a turn-off to white industrialists seemed inescapable.

Progress in Spite of Setbacks

In the months since my research ended, I have witnessed both political progress and setbacks for black Southerners. One of the chapters of my book, *Free at Last*, focused on Robert Clark, the first

122

black Mississippi legislator in modern times. In 1982 and 1984, Clark ran for Congress in the Second District of Mississippi—a district with a majority black population. In 1982 the voting-age population was nearly 50 percent black, and by 1984 it was more than 50 percent black. All Clark needed to win was a strong black turnout and a smattering of white support. In the end, he did not get enough of either.

On election night 1986, however, Mike Espy, a former consumer protection lawyer in the attorney general's office in Mississippi, stunned observers by achieving what Clark had failed to do in the Second District. He became Mississippi's first black congressman in this century and a sign of indisputable progress.

If that chapter of my book was originally too pessimistic, another chapter may have been too optimistic. It focused on Harvey Gantt, the former mayor of Charlotte, North Carolina. Charlotte is 70 percent white, and Gantt, along with Doug Wilder, was the most prominent example of a Southern black politician elected with substantial white votes. However, in a defeat that few saw coming, Gantt was turned out in November 1987 in voting that closely followed racial lines. His conclusions: that blacks elected with white votes must be ever vigilant, and that white voters are far less forgiving of mistakes by black officials than by white officials.

And so, as Southern blacks embarked on their third decade of political power, much remained to be done. There had been tremendous strides, but Lyndon Johnson's promise still awaited fulfillment. In the years after the Voting Rights Act took effect, numbers were the test. Each new face on the roster of black elected officials signaled victory. What those sheriffs, commissioners, and registrars achieved was less important than that they existed at all. As a new decade began, the broader question was one of performance—whether black officials could help shape a fairer, more successful social welfare policy; whether the economic gulf dividing poor blacks from other Southerners might somehow be bridged; whether the inner cities and isolated counties where many

123

blacks held office might be blended into the whole of Southern life.

Change is evolutionary, and the challenge of the 1990s—except for an isolated Sunflower County here and there—is no longer to elect black officials. It is to ensure that votes make a lasting impact on economics—a task that seems as gargantuan as giving blacks votes that counted once did, but without which the American story and the Negro story cannot finally fuse and blend.

Notes

1. On March 7, 1965, several hundred demonstrators were viciously attacked by state troopers and police officers as they began a voter registration march from Selma to Montgomery, Alabama. The march, completed several days later, was a turning point in alerting the nation to the need for voting rights legislation.

2. In April 1985 I conducted telephone interviews with officials in offices of the county commission or circuit clerk in majority black counties in the states originally covered by the Voting Rights Act. The data collected during these interviews showed that the following counties had no black commissioners: Dallas and Marengo Counties in Alabama; Calhoun, Macon, Randolph, Stewart, Taliafero, Washington, and Webster Counties in Georgia; Jefferson Davis, Kemper, Sunflower, Tallahatchie, and Washington Counties in Mississippi; and Gates County in North Carolina.

3. In 1989 Douglas Wilder was elected governor of Virginia—the first black governor anywhere in the nation since Reconstruction.

4. U.S. Department of Commerce, Bureau of the Census, Census of the Population, 1980. "Alabama—General Social and Economic Characteristics" (Washington, D.C.: GPO), Report No. PC-80-1-C2.

5. Joint Center for Political and Economic Studies, "Black Elected Officials in the United States, January 1985," in *Focus*, Vol. 13 (May 1985), pp. 4-5.

6. I derived this figure from statistics provided by the Joint Center for Political and Economic Studies and from interviews with public officials representing secretaries of state, associations of county commissioners, state municipal leagues, and others in each of the seven states.

7. See note 2.

8. Pat Watters and Reese Cleghorn, *Climbing Jacob's Ladder* (New York: Harcourt, Brace and World), pp. 376-77.

9. U.S. Department of Commerce, Bureau of the Census, Current Population Reports. "Voting and Registration in the Election of 1984" (Advance Report) (Washington: GPO, January 1985): P-20, 397.

10. Watters and Cleghorn, *Climbing Jacob's Ladder*.

11. U.S. Department of Commerce, "Voting and Registration in the Election of 1984."

12. *Ibid.*

13. In January 1967, marchers protesting the absence of any black residents in Forsyth County (about 30 miles north of Atlanta)

were attacked by onlookers. Ninety marchers were injured, and eight attackers were arrested.

14. Among those indicted were Albert Turner, a pallbearer at Martin Luther King's funeral and an organizer of Selma's "Bloody Sunday" march; his wife, Evelyn; and Councilman Spiver Gordon of Eutaw, Alabama, the former head of the Greene County Civic League.

15. This information was gleaned from an interview I conducted on February 26, 1985, with Rodney Strong, the acting director of the Office of Contract Compliance for the City of Atlanta.

16. The following counties had a higher unemployment rate than average: Marengo County in Alabama; Calhoun, Clay, Greene, and Randolph Counties in Georgia; Gates County in North Carolina; Calhoun, Edgefield, Hampton, and McCormick Counties in South Carolina; Clay, Madison, and Yazoo Counties in Mississippi; and Sussex County in Virginia.

Although women and blacks remain underrepresented, voting patterns and recent gains suggest that the future will bring greater numbers of women and blacks into political office and that women will continue to vote at higher rates than men.

Muted Voices: A Comparative Perspective of Women's and Blacks' Voting Participation

Celinda Lake

In the United States, sex and race have had a similar impact on voting participation. Women and blacks share both a history of exclusion from the centers of American political power and a position disproportionately on the fringes of the economy. Only recently have they voted at a rate comparable to their white male counterparts, and they still lag significantly in electoral mobilization as measured by their running for and holding political office.

This exploratory essay compares the political participation of women and blacks in this century. It briefly reviews the history of their voting participation, underscoring the importance of internal ideological constraints for women and of external institutional barriers for blacks. It suggests that the dynamics of enfranchisement—particularly the need to develop the "habit of voting"—illuminate complex interactions of sex, race, age, and occupation as determinants of voting participation. Finally, it presents a discussion of the implications of voting patterns and partisan differences and their effect on representation and empowerment as we enter the 1990s.

A Brief History of the Women's Vote

The granting of women's suffrage in the Nineteenth Amendment to the Constitution did not send them flocking to the polls. Most historians agree that in the presidential election of 1920, well under half the eligible women voted; Ethel Klein, for example, estimates that one-third of the women eligible to vote nationally actually cast ballots that year.[1]

Women were most likely to vote in the West and the Northeast; in Vermont and Chicago, for instance, about 40 percent of eligible women were registered.[2] Higher turnout in the West and Northeast correlated strongly with women's more equal economic participation in those regions and with their involvement in local politics, even before suffrage was granted. In the South, participation among women was lower; for example, fewer than 20 percent of eligible women were registered in Louisiana.[3] This reflected the unique culture of the South as well as lower levels of education for most women.

After 1920, women's participation at the polls increased— gradually at first, then rapidly during the 1960s. By World War II, turnout among women was about 50 percent; by 1948 it had risen to 59 percent. Prior to 1960, men's participation significantly exceeded women's; but by 1968, two-thirds of eligible women went to the polls, and the gap had closed. Turnout among men in 1968 was 69 percent—only three percentage points higher than turnout among women. And by 1980, women in every racial group voted and registered in higher numbers than men.[4]

Low participation rates for women can be explained in part by internal ideological constraints. Supporters of women's suffrage were far from unified regarding support of equal rights for women or of broader social transformation. Rather, suffragists were split into two factions: those who were principled proponents of equal political rights for women, and those who hoped that suffrage would allow women to expand their housekeeping role to benefit society more generally.[5] This split was manifested in early twentieth-century legal struggles; on one side were those who demanded that women be treated equally by the law, and on the other side were those who argued that women were entitled to special protection. The same split was evident in the more recent fight over the Equal Rights Amendment: Many who believed women should be entitled to equal opportunity under the law nonetheless feared that the amendment would eliminate important protections.[6]

These internal constraints on women's participation continue to affect the woman's vote. Until recently, many women did not vote because they did not perceive voting as part of their proper role in society. With their diminished sense that they had the power— or even the right—to influence the world around them, women had less interest in voting. A remnant of these barriers is particularly evident in the lower turnout of women who do not work outside the home. Early work by Kent Jennings illustrates this dynamic. Jennings found that women's participation is highly correlated to the relevance of politics in their daily lives. For example, women traditionally have participated at higher rates than men in school board elections—even before their overall voting participation increased. It is no coincidence, therefore, that women began to seek a significant political role at the same time they assumed a significant economic role outside the household.[7]

A Brief History of the Black Vote

Black Americans formally were granted the right to vote long before women. However, as the civil rights movement made painfully clear, blacks (particularly Southern blacks) were systematically and violently denied the right to vote through physical intimidation and coercion as well as through legal obstructions. In contrast to the internal barriers that hindered early participation by women, the primary deterrents to immediate black participation were institutional and physical. In real terms, then, black suffrage only became meaningful with the passage of the Voting Rights Act of 1965.

131

This act had a dramatic effect on black participation. Between 1965 and 1985, black registration in the South more than doubled, increasing from 31 percent of eligible blacks registered in 1965 to 66 percent in 1985. In Louisiana, Mississippi, and South Carolina, blacks were registered in greater proportions than whites in 1985.[8]

Although black registration and turnout may have leveled off with the 1988 election, as recently as 1984 there was a major surge in registration and turnout among blacks, reflecting both organized efforts and the mobilizing effect of black candidacies for national and local office. Nationally, 60 percent of eligible blacks were registered to vote in 1980, 66.3 percent in 1984. Turnout among blacks was 50.5 percent in 1980, 55.8 percent in 1984.[9]

Full mobilization of black voters, however, has not been achieved. In 1984 there was more than a 10-point gap between registration and turnout among blacks—the highest for any racial group. In part this reflects the recent surge in newly registered black voters, since new registrants generally turn out at lower rates.[10]

Factors Affecting Women's Participation

Among both men and women, the primary determinants of voting are socioeconomic variables: education, income, and occupation.[11] However, while the relationship of education and income to women's voting is fairly direct, the impact of occupation is more complex and reflects the effects of a woman's education and income as well as her prevailing attitudes.

Among employed women, professionals are the most likely to vote, blue-collar workers the least likely. However, one of the most important determinants of a woman's participation is whether she has joined the work force at all: Women who do not work outside the home continue to vote less often than most women who are employed.[12]

The effect of employment has at least two explanations. First, women who work outside the home are more likely to have accumulated the education and experience that increase voting participation among all groups, male and female. They show more interest in national and state politics, and they feel they can exercise greater efficacy in influencing policy.

Second, and perhaps equally important, women who do not work also may remain more committed to an older social ideology, which explains both a choice not to work outside the home and a choice not to vote.[13] In fact, as more women have entered the paid work force at least on a part-time basis, types of work make as much difference in voting participation and attitudes as does entry into the work force itself. Women who work in domestic and traditionally female occupations have come increasingly to resemble those who still work at home.

Finally, Southern women generally have been less likely to vote than Northern women, even after controlling for demographic differences. Authors Earl and Merle Black suggest that, even more than in other regions, increasing the educational level has boosted women's voting participation in the South.[14] Only recently have participation rates of Southern women approached those of Northern women and of men.[15]

The Interaction of Gender and Race

In general, the same variables that predict turnout generally and women's turnout in particular also predict black turnout, both male and female: education, income, and occupation. In fact, for blacks with incomes over $10,000, the differences between black and white turnout overall can be explained entirely by these demographic differences. But there is also a significant gender gap in turnout among black voters. While turnout and registration among white women has overtaken turnout and registration among white men only recently, black women have led participation in the black community since 1976. In 1972 turnout and registration of black men and women was about equal; in 1976 turnout and registration of black women surpassed that of black men by about three percentage points. By 1984 the percentage of black women voting

133

exceeded that of black men by more than seven points; only black women over 65 years old register and vote at lower rates than their male counterparts.[16]

Moreover, while blacks as a group are less likely than whites to register and vote, since 1984 black women have registered and voted in proportions equal to white men. In 1984, 59.2 percent of black women reported voting, compared to 60.8 percent of white men; that same year, 69.5 percent of black women were registered to vote, compared to 68.9 percent of white men. After controlling for occupation, income, and education, black women participate at higher rates than their male counterparts, both white and black.[17]

In fact, black women are more likely than men or whites generally to have political attitudes that contribute to voting participation. Black women are the most apt to seek a way to redistribute power in our society, to believe that women and blacks have too little economic and political power, to have developed a sense of group consciousness, and to see political power in systemic terms.[18]

The Habit of Voting and the Effect of Age

In addition to overcoming ideological and institutional barriers to voting, newly enfranchised groups in the United States have had to develop the "habit of voting," a pattern of behavior acquired both by individuals and groups over time by regularly practicing the act of voting.

The importance of the habit of voting becomes evident when one analyzes the relationship between age and voting participation. Older people generally vote at higher rates than younger people, in part because older people have developed the individual habit of voting.[19] Yet when any group first achieves suffrage, the older members of that group have actually acquired the habit of not voting, which depresses the group's participation for a period of time. This has been true for both blacks and women.

Successive generations, or cohorts, also reflect the experience

134

of changing social conditions. Thus, while older people are more likely than younger voters to register and vote among every racial group, it is the voting patterns of younger women that produce the edge over men in both registration and turnout, because of the social revolution in women's lives and their growing educational and employment levels. In 1984, for example, the gap in registration between younger and older women (both black and white) was considerably smaller than the gap between younger and older men: about 22 percentage points for women, more than 30 points for men. In other words, while older women are less likely to vote than older men, younger women are more likely to vote than younger men.[20] As this cohort ages, we can expect the gender gap in registration and turnout to become even larger.

There is similar evidence of growth in the habit of voting among blacks. While younger blacks register and vote in about the same proportions as younger whites, older blacks are substantially less likely to register and vote than older whites. In 1984, for instance, 61.5 percent of blacks over 65 years old reported voting, compared to 67.7 percent of all voters over 65. Even more striking, there appears to be a direct interaction between race, sex, and age: Younger black women are among those most likely to register and vote; older black women are among the least likely.[21]

Participation and Representation

As voting participation by women and blacks has increased, holding elected office has become an even more telling measure of their lack of full participation in our system. Although the number of women and black officeholders has increased significantly in the last 20 years, the disparity between population and representation remains stark. In 1985, for example, blacks represented 26 percent of Southerners but only 8 to 10 percent of the South's elected officials.[22] Today, although blacks constitute approximately 13 percent of the American population, less than 4 percent of the members of Congress are black.

135

The disparity for women in 1988 is even greater. A majority of American voters are female, but there are only 27 women in Congress—less than five percent. Women represent 15 percent of state legislators, and only two governors are women. Among black elected officials, one-fifth are women, and both black and white women officeholders are concentrated in lower level and local offices. Only one black woman serves in Congress.

These inequities take on added importance in light of the striking partisan and policy differences between men and women and between blacks and whites. About 80 percent of all black voters currently are Democrats. Although the imbalance between women and men is smaller than between blacks and whites (most polls show that women are about seven points more Democratic), the women's vote made the difference in close elections. In 1986, for example, the votes of women and blacks returned control of the Senate to the Democrats by providing the margin of victory in nine key races.[23] And in 1988 a majority of men and women disagreed over who should be President: According to ABC exit polls, 54 percent of men supported George Bush, while 52 percent of women supported Michael Dukakis.

Women's policy preferences also differ markedly from men's. Public opinion surveys consistently show that women feel much more economically marginal than men. Women are more apt to want change, and they are more likely to want the government to play a role in producing that change. In contrast, men tend to be more comfortable with the status quo.

As a result, women tend to be more supportive of policies of "compassion" and domestic policy intervention. For example, women are more likely to support social welfare programs, a government role in the economy, and government regulation to protect the environment. At the same time, women tend to reject policies involving risk and physical force. Women consistently have been less willing to get involved in military conflicts, use the death penalty, increase defense spending, or invest in nuclear power and weapons.[24]

136

Perspective on the Future

Although women and blacks remain underrepresented, voting patterns and recent gains suggest that the future will bring greater numbers of women and blacks into political office and that women will continue to vote at higher rates than men. In addition to changing social norms, which fuel expectations (if not yet achievement) of political equality, voting participation of women and blacks is likely to increase as today's young cohort grows older and as new young voters enter the electorate. In addition, the tendency of both women and black voters to respond in greater numbers to the candidacies of their peers may take on added importance as women and blacks increasingly seek higher offices.[25]

A central question is whether greater participation and representation of blacks and women will bring changes in policy and government. Women and—to an even greater extent—blacks have policy needs and views significantly at variance with those of white men. As officeholders, blacks and women have differed from white men markedly in the policies they have introduced.[26] As women and blacks achieve greater economic integration, their attitudinal gaps may close. If, on the other hand, serious economic disparities continue, the gaps may widen further and the growing empowerment of blacks and women–at the polls and in political office—may bring political transformation on a dramatic scale.

Notes

1. Ethel Klein, *Gender Politics* (Cambridge: Harvard University Press, 1984), p. 142.

2. Chicago, however, granted women the vote for presidential elections in 1913. In 1914, 32 percent of eligible women were registered to vote there. See Virginia Sapiro, *The Political Integration of Women* (Urbana: University of Illinois Press, 1983).

137

3. Sandra Baxter and Marjorie Lansing, *Women and Politics: The Visible Majority* (Ann Arbor: University of Michigan Press, 1983), p. 21.

4. See American Citizenship Education Project (ACEP), "The Changing Face of the American Electorate" (Washington, D.C.: ACEP, 1988). It should be noted, however, that the relative increase in women's voting participation was not steady. For example, according to the ACEP, in 1964 the gap between women's and men's turnout was greater than in 1960.

5. Joan Hoff-Wilson, "The Unfinished Revolution: Changing Legal Status of U.S. Women," in *Signs*, Vol. 13 (1987), pp. 7-36.

6. Jane J. Mansbridge, *Why We Lost the ERA* (Chicago: University of Chicago Press, 1986).

7. See also M. Kent Jennings, "Gender Roles and Inequalities in Political Participation: Results from an Eight-Nation Study," in *Western Political Quarterly*, Vol. 36 (1983), pp. 364-85.

8. Margaret Edds, *Free at Last* (Bethesda, Maryland: Adler & Adler, 1987), pp. 11-12.

9. ACEP, "The Changing Face of the American Electorate."

10. *Ibid.* Among whites, the gap between registration and turnout was about eight points; among voters of Hispanic origin, the gap was 7.5 points.

11. Baxter and Lansing, *Women and Politics*; Raymond Wolfinger and Steven Rosenstone, *Who Votes* (New Haven: Yale University Press, 1980).

12. Kristi Andersen, "Working Women and Political Participation, 1952-1974," in *American Journal of Political Science*, Vol. 19 (1975), pp. 439-455; Keith T. Poole and L. Harmon Zeigler, *Women, Public Opinion, and Politics: The Changing Political Attitudes of American Women* (White Plains, New York: Longman Press, 1985); E. Witt, "What the Republicans Have Learned about Women," in *Public Opinion*, Vol. 8 (October-November 1985), pp. 49-57; Susan Welch, "Women as Political Animals? A Test of Some Explanations of Male-Female Participation Differences," in *American Journal of Political Science*, Vol. 21 (1977), pp. 714-15.

It should be noted, however, that women with blue-collar jobs vote even less often than women who have remained in the home.

13. Although Sapiro (see note 2) argues that it is not employment per se that influences the likelihood of voting but rather women's interpretations of their roles, homemakers are more likely to interpret their roles as "private" ones than women in the paid work force.

14. Earl and Merle Black, *Politics and Society in the South* (Cambridge: Harvard University Press, 1987).

15. Baxter and Lansing, *Women and Politics*, p. 32.

16. Among white voters, this gap was only 1.2 percent; among Hispanic voters, the gap was one percent.

17. Linda Faye Williams, "Black Female Political Empowerment: A Plan for Self Help," Joint Center for Political Studies working paper (August 1986).

18. *Ibid.*

19. Older people have also acquired more life experiences, which have a function similar to education in determining voting. Therefore, the elderly are more likely to be integrated into their communities.

20. ACEP, "The Changing Face of the American Electorate."

21. *Ibid.*

22. Edds, *Free At Last.*

23. Celinda Lake and Nikki Heidepriem, "Whatever Happened to the Gender Gap?," in *Campaigns and Elections* (March-April 1988), pp. 37-40.

24. See, for example, Kathleen Frankovic, "Sex and Politics-New Alignments, Old Issues," in *PS*, Vol. 15 (1982), pp. 439-448; Robert Y. Shapiro and Harpreet Mahajan, "Gender Differences in Policy Preferences: A Summary of Trends from the 1960s to the 1980s," in *Public Opinion Quarterly*, Vol. 50 (1986), pp. 42-61; and Tom W. Smith, "The Polls: Gender and Attitudes toward Violence," in *Public Opinion Quarterly*, Vol. 48 (1984), pp. 384-96.

25. For example, the Reverend Jesse Jackson has been credited with greatly increasing black turnout and registration nationally, as was Chicago Mayor Harold Washington locally. Similarly, we know that women, who tend to make up their minds later in the campaign season, decide earlier when women candidates are on the ticket.

26. R. Darcy, Susan Welch, and Janet Clark, *Women, Elections, and Representation* (White Plains, New York: Longman Press, 1987).

Citizen Action
in Voting

Sometimes we get so engrossed in trying to change the details of the system that we forget we can change the system altogether.

State Initiatives to Increase Voter Participation

Bill Clinton *

Voting rights in America are a hidden resource for our nation's poor and downtrodden. Too many of us take our right to vote for granted, not aware that others among us have not been so fortunate. Some have never been taught the value of voting; others have met with unconcern or downright hostility when they try to register; still others have grown disaffected when the votes they cast seem to have no discernible effect. It is these neglected and frustrated Americans that we must work assiduously to bring into the election system.

When I ran for governor of Arkansas during the height of a nationwide recession in 1982, our state and region were confronting several critical issues including high unemployment, high interest rates, phasing out of revenue sharing, and pruning back of Social Security for children. Our citizens' safety net was badly torn and needed immediate repair. In such a climate of despair perhaps it is not surprising that our state garnered a bigger turnout of black voters

---

* The author wishes to reiterate that the following essay is based on a speech given at the 1988 conference, sponsored by the Leadership Conference Education Fund, on the bicentennial celebration of the U.S. Constitution.

143

during that off-year election than had voted in the previous presidential election—something that had never happened before.

But despite gains of political power by black voters, effective political power remains beyond the reach not only of ordinary voters but of people who might be expected to represent them in various political offices on various issues. Fortunately, this situation is changing. More and more elected officials in our region—without regard to race or political philosophy—are coming to terms with the underlying difficulties we face. Nevertheless, significant barriers to effective participation in the political process still exist.

The Framers of our nation's Constitution gave states the right to prescribe their own qualifications for voting because, as James Madison said, it is difficult to form any uniform rules that would apply equally to all states; therefore, he argued, the states are the best judges of the circumstances and temperament of their people. Today, however, I question whether people believe that axiom.

I would like to address the following questions:
- How have various states expanded the franchise, either on their own initiative or because they were sued and forced to comply?
- What still needs to be done?
- What can groups like the Leadership Conference on Civil Rights, the NAACP Legal Defense Fund, the League of Women Voters, and others do to encourage greater action on the home front?

Citizenship in a Global Era

It is important to recognize that we do have a significant problem with international economic competition. The Europeans and the Japanese are relatively as wealthy as we are. We Americans must readjust our attitudes considerably if we hope to remain competitive in the world economy that is now emerging. One of the first things we must do is to guarantee that our citizenship is as effective as that of other nations.

In the most recent presidential election in France, for example, nearly 85 percent of the eligible voters went to the polls on election day.[1] In America there aren't more than two states that ever have an 80 percent turnout, even during a presidential election when interest runs very high.[2]

In 1984 the United States witnessed the largest voter registration effort in two decades—12 million voters were registered. This meant 61 percent of those eligible were registered; yet only about 53 percent of them voted.[3] The numbers show that we are still a long way from participatory democracy in this nation.

There are still too many cumbersome and outdated administrative impediments standing in the way of voting rights. Efforts underway to remove these barriers have met with mixed success.

Out of frustration with the checkerboard pattern of development from state to state, Senator Alan Cranston of California has introduced a bill in the Senate. Among the cosponsors is Senator Quentin Burdick of North Dakota, the only state that does not require voter registration. All you need do there is show up at the polls on election day and vote. (One might argue convincingly that such a system works only in a very rural, sparsely populated state where officials already may know 80 percent of the 650,000 residents by their first names.)

Senator Cranston's bill, S. 2061, the Universal Voter Registration Act of 1988, mandates three methods of registering voters: election-day registration, currently allowed by only three states (in addition to North Dakota, where registration is not necessary); registration by mail, presently found in only 23 states and the District of Columbia even though it has been an option to states since 1941, when it was adopted by Texas; and agency-based registration, subject to design by the states affected.[4]

I believe it would be useful to review how each of these three methods is faring in various states.

Election-Day Registration. Maine, Minnesota, and Wisconsin are the three states that permit voter registration on election day.

Since 1972, when election-day registration was first adopted, voter turnout rose by eight percent, a significant increase in the states that adopted it. During the 1984 election, the Federal Election Commission found that Minnesota ranked first among states in voting participation, Maine was second, and Wisconsin was fourth.[5] The Minnesota Secretary of State reports that more than 90 percent of the state's eligible voters are registered;[6] generally, 5 to 10 percent of those voters register on election day just before they vote. Of course, other factors apart from election-day registration might have contributed to this increase, but there is no question that election-day registration has played a major role.

No significant evidence has arisen to suggest that election-day registration has any substantial effect on the political composition of the electorate or that it has exacerbated voter fraud. Should someone suspect that a fraudulent ballot has been cast, it can be challenged and will not be counted until after the validity of the voter's registration has been confirmed.

New York Governor Mario Cuomo's Task Force on Voter Registration recommended in March 1988 that election-day registration be implemented in that state. New York is far more economically, culturally, and politically diverse than the other three states that permit election-day registration. Thus, if adopted and successful there, New York's initiative would give great impetus to the rest of the country to follow suit.

Registration by Mail. Twenty-three states allow registration by mail. Many other states have tried unsuccessfully to institute this method. In 1987 my administration supported a bill to implement postcard voter registration in Arkansas, but the bill never got out of committee because legislators feared it would promote fraud.

Such dire predictions appear groundless. Several states have watched voter participation soar after they adopted postcard registration. When Alaska shifted to postcard registration, the registered population increased by more than 20 percent, while voter turnout increased by more than 9 percent. In the District of

Columbia, postcard registration reversed a persistent decline in registered voters and voter turnout. In Iowa, the number of registered voters increased by 14 percent between 1976 and 1980 after the state went to postcard registration.

Moreover, remarkably few problems have been reported. Ohio, which has a relatively liberal set of rules, did find a single case of fraud: A state legislator voted illegally! He alleged that he was just trying to test the system, and he was glad to discover that it worked.

Registration by State Agencies. One of the most important initiatives of recent years is the idea of agency-based registration; in other words, using state agencies that come in contact with people traditionally underrepresented in the electorate to help register them. In Arkansas we have begun to register people through our Department of Human Services offices. Although we started only a few months ago [i.e., in 1988], it is clear that many people will register now who did not understand how the system works or where they were supposed to register—people who never had occasion to go into the county courthouse but who do come in contact with our Department of Human Services personnel.[7]

The same process is evolving in many other states. There are agency-based registrations by law or through executive orders in Idaho, Montana, New York, Ohio, and Texas. Governor Rudy Perpich of Minnesota has asked his agency directors to consider implementing agency-based registration. West Virginia and New Mexico have authorized their Departments of Human Services to register voters in branch offices. Twenty-one executives or mayors have also directed agencies dealing with low-income people to register voters. Maryland, Washington, and Illinois have passed legislation authorizing various types of registration by agency.

Several states are beginning to register voters through revenue offices on the theory that at least everybody who has a car should be a registered voter. Michigan has a "motor-voter" registration program and is using its 180 branch offices to register voters.[8] Ten thousand New York voters were registered during a two-week

147

period through agency registration; in Ohio 70,000 voters were registered over a two-month period. Obviously, agency registration works.

Administrative Barriers to Voting

Another initiative that has been discussed by states involves purging the voters' names from the rolls. In 1987 I signed a law requiring that voters be notified before their names are removed from the rolls. Prior to that, you were taken off the rolls if you hadn't voted within the last four years. An outmoded assumption allegedly designed to prevent fraud, I believe the real idea behind it was that if you weren't going to vote, you shouldn't retain the right to continue voting unless you went to the trouble of registering again. We have changed that dynamic in Arkansas, and I sincerely hope many other states will follow suit.

Michigan, Maryland, South Carolina, and Rhode Island have introduced computerized solutions to various administrative barriers found in those states. Minnesota is now sending voter registration materials along with tax forms. The thinking goes that when people receive their tax materials, they get so incensed that they'll register immediately if they hadn't already!

As of 1988 several states are introducing other kinds of reforms: New Hampshire, Georgia, Louisiana, Indiana, and Mississippi (the latter under a court order) are considering legislation to allow more accessible registration.[9] Minnesota and other states are considering options like telephone voting for handicapped and homebound elderly people. I think it is imperative that disabled and immobilized citizens be able to register and vote from home through a computer device.

How States Can Facilitate Voting Registration

Individual states, then, are making progress. So the question becomes: Have we done enough to facilitate registration? Does it make sense to accept such wide variations in practice from state to state? If not, two options exist: (1) We can support federal action

148

in this area, or (2) we can devise alternative state-based methods of implementing more consistent action among states. One of the ideas I have suggested is that the National Governors Association be urged to adopt a uniform policy. Should that occur, many governors who had never given much consideration to this issue would spend a lot more time thinking about it and trying to move it along. I would also like to see an effort to get the National Governors Association, the National Council of State Legislatures, and the National Association of Counties on record in favor of some basic, uniform principles of voter registration. Their support would lend great weight to this issue.

Another significant barrier to our economic security, social stability, and greater political participation is the enormous number of functionally illiterate adults in our nation today. This issue now receives far greater attention than it did just a few years ago, and it is increasingly being seen as an integral part of any educational reform or economic development program. We will experience real frustration in our efforts to increase voter participation in traditionally underrepresented groups unless we make a concomitant effort to reduce the barriers that illiteracy imposes. We can help eliminate these barriers by simplifying voting procedures and by simultaneously increasing the literacy levels of our people.

With a carefully designed plan, and a commitment from the president on down, we could dramatically reduce the illiteracy rate among working-age Americans. If that were accomplished, I believe we would see an enormous increase in voter participation throughout this nation.

One final point: Many nations around the world don't vote during working hours on working days. If you really want to go from 50 percent to 80 percent voting participation; if you want to attract people who work in low-paying jobs and who can't simply walk off the job to vote without being fired; if you want to draw factory workers who leave for work at 5:30 a.m. and who, though they may have time to vote when they get off work, may also be dead tired and have to pick up three kids on the way home, we might have to consider whether we want to keep the polls open longer, vote over two days, or even vote over an entire weekend. There is no doubt that we could have a substantial increase in voter participation if we changed the day or lengthened the time for voting. Sometimes we get so engrossed in trying to change the details of the system that we forget we can change the system altogether.

The Path to True Democracy

Our country will benefit immeasurably by debating these issues of voting rights as we enter the twenty-first century. We will live in a world that is more competitive, more uncertain, and ever fuller of catalytic change. The average eighteen-year-old, it is predicted, will change jobs eight times in a lifetime. We are going to become more racially and culturally diverse. It will become more difficult to preserve the idea of the United States of America. For, fundamentally, that's what this country is—an idea. It is not a race. It is not a fixed set of institutions. It is a grand idea that has been implanted in our minds and embodied in our Constitution. As change accelerates, diversity explodes, and our nation inevitably metamorphoses, we will be hard pressed to find a shared set of core values and a system that can surmount these obstacles. We must create new bonds to hold our nation together. One way to do that is to develop a system in which 80 percent instead of 50 percent of the people participate on election day.

To reach that goal of 80 percent voter participation, we must tear down the remaining barriers to participation. Our government at every level must promote rather than discourage participation. Those of us in government sometimes have other issues on our minds; some of us may even feel threatened by the prospect of increased voter participation. Therefore, everyone who cares about expanding American democracy should apply steady pressure on public officials to make sure we in government take whatever actions are necessary to throw open the doors to the polls.

Therein lies the path to true democracy in America.

Notes

1. National Governors Association Resolution No. A-29, unanimously passed on February 28, 1989.

2. *Ibid.*

3. *Ibid.*

4. Memorandum to Governor Bill Clinton from the Leadership Conference on Civil Rights, People for the American Way, the Mexican Legal Defense and Education Fund, HumanServe, and the NAACP Legal and Education Fund, Inc., page 2.

5. *Ibid.*, page 3.

6. From a conversation with staff of the Minnesota secretary of state.

7. This effort, begun in 1988, is still under way in Arkansas as of 1992.

8. Memorandum to Governor Clinton (see note 4), page 3.

9. *Ibid.*, page 3.

There is a growing awareness among Indians that they have the potential to influence policy as well as local and regional elections.

Native American Political Participation

Jeanette Wolfley

To fully examine the political participation of Native Americans in this country, one must look to constitutional provisions and to the unique and complex history of the legal status of Native Americans. Basically, the struggle for voting rights mirrors the larger clash of Indian and white cultures. The history of the Indian franchise contains a panoply of shifting white attitudes towards Indians. Indeed, federal policies first sought to isolate and relocate Indian tribes to Indian country outside state limits but later sought to assimilate Indians into the dominant white society.

This paper first examines the struggle of Indians to gain the rights of citizenship and to vote. It then discusses the various voting barriers employed by states to disenfranchise Indians. Finally, it reviews the current political participation of Indians.

Historical Relationship between the Tribes and the United States

It is a fundamental principle of federal Indian law that a government-to-government relationship exists between Indian tribes and the United States. Nearly 400 treaties and an entire title of the United States Code are premised on this relationship. The relationship is similar to that between foreign nations and the United States.[1]

Although the Constitution is often cited as the source for the government-to-government interaction between the tribes and the

United States, the relationship actually predates the Constitution.[2] Tribal governments existed for centuries before the arrival of Europeans on this continent; and upon contact with the new settlers, these tribal governments engaged in war, commerce, and other activities with non-Indian governments. Thus, the relationship is rooted in international law.[3]

The first court decisions dealing with Indians treated the tribes as distinct and independent political communities with the right of self-government.[4] Further, tribes were not subject to any state law[5] but were dealt with exclusively by Congress.[6] Thus, prior to 1871,[7] most Indians were considered to be members of separate political communities and not part of the state politic or the United States.

Indians' Lack of Citizenship

To be eligible to vote in the United States, one must be a citizen. Prior to the adoption of the Fourteenth Amendment in 1868, there was no definition of citizenship in the Constitution. The Fourteenth Amendment declared, "All persons born or naturalized in the United States and subject to the jurisdiction thereof, are citizens of the United States and of the State wherein they reside." Interpreted literally, this definition should have made Indians citizens. However, an Oregon district court held that the Fourteenth Amendment did not apply to Indians.[8] The court declared:

> To be a citizen of the United States by reason of his birth, a person must not only be born within its territorial limits, but he must also be born subject to its juris-diction—that is, in its power and obedience. . . . But the Indian tribes within the limits of the United States have always been held to be distinct and independent political communities, retaining the right of self-government, though subject to the protecting power of the United States.[9]

In 1884 in *Elk* v. *Wilkins*,[10] the Supreme Court confirmed the exclusion of Indians from the franchise. John Elk, an Indian

154

residing in Omaha and apart from his Indian tribe, attempted to vote in Nebraska in 1880. The Court reasoned that the Fifteenth Amendment, which extends the right to vote to all citizens, did not apply to Mr. Elk. Moreover, he was not considered a citizen within the meaning of the Fourteenth Amendment's phrase "born . . . subject to the jurisdiction . . . of the United States." Rather, Mr. Elk was born under tribal authority.[11] The Court also inferred from the phrase "Indians not taxed" in Section 2 of the Fourteenth Amendment that the drafters did not intend the amendment to apply to Indians.[12] Additionally, the dictum of *United States* v. *Wong Kim Ark*[13] excepted from its doctrine of citizenship by birth "children of Indian tribes owing direct allegiance to their several tribes."

Naturalization of Indians from the 1880s to the 1920s

In the late nineteenth century, it became a federal policy to encourage Indians to abandon their tribal relations and to adopt the life and customs of "civilization." To this end, in 1871 Congress ended treaty-making with Indian tribes and enacted special laws to provide for allotment of lands to individual Indians.[14] As a further inducement to abandon their tribal status, Indians to whom such allotments were granted were made citizens of the United States.

For example, the General Allotment Act of 1887[15] conferred citizenship upon two classes of Indians born within the United States: (1) those to whom allotments were made by law or treaty; and (2) those who voluntarily lived apart from their tribes and "adopted the habits of civilized life." Other statutes such as the Act of August 9, 1888, granted citizenship to any Indian woman married to a white man,[16] and citizenship was granted to particular tribes.[17]

The Act of May 8, 1906, also known as the Burke Act,[18] declared that an Indian became a citizen after a patent in fee was granted instead of the completion of his allotment and issuance of a trust patent. (A trust patent refers to land that is held in trust by the United States for the benefit of the Indian; there are restrictions placed on the land, such as no taxes and no encumbrances, and it is

155

inalienable. A patent in fee, on the other hand, is land held without any restrictions by the individual Indian.) An Indian was considered a citizen under the Burke Act because the conveyance of the fee patent was also an adjudication that the Indian was "competent and capable" to manage his own affairs.[19]

It was not until World War I that Congress saw fit to attempt to solve the issue of Indian citizenship. During World War I, many Indians volunteered both for service in the armed forces and for war work on the home front, including people whose tribes had been fighting the United States as recently as 35 years before. As a result of the Indian response to the national emergency, it became apparent that the federal government finally would have to respond to the ambiguity of Indians' legal status. In 1919 Congress declared that all Indians who had served in the armed forces and had received honorable discharges could be granted American citizenship upon application.[20]

Prior to World War I, Woodrow Wilson's Secretary of the Interior Franklin Lane identified the political potential inherent in the Indian as a voter, particularly in the Dakotas, Arizona, New Mexico, Montana, Oklahoma, and other states with a relatively large number of Indians in otherwise sparsely settled rural areas. Secretary Lane urged the Democratic Party to seek to enroll Indian voters in the 1916 national election. However, most non-Indians in the western states were quite hostile to the idea of Indians as voters, even though Indians would have been participating only in federal elections.

Both the Harding and Coolidge administrations were well aware of the political potential of the Indian voter and moved in the direction of increasing Indian participation in the political decision-making process. As a result, in 1924 Congress passed the Indian Citizenship Act, which stated the following:

> That all noncitizen Indians born within the territorial limits of the United States be, and they are hereby, declared to be citizens of the United States: Provided

that the granting of such citizenship not in any manner impair or otherwise affect the right of any Indian to tribal or other property.[21]

The drafter of the Citizenship Act was Charles Curtis, a Kaw Indian from Oklahoma who served in the U.S. House of Representatives from 1893 to 1907 and in the U.S. Senate from 1907 to 1913 and again from 1915 to 1929. Curtis later served as vice president to Herbert Hoover. It has been estimated that approximately two-thirds of the Indians in the United States had acquired citizenship prior to 1924 under treaties and other laws.

State Barriers to Citizenship

Even though the question of United States citizenship was settled in 1924, some states still refused to recognize Indians as citizens of the states in which they resided. State action to deny Indians their franchise was no surprise given the history of antagonism between Indian tribes and states. The Supreme Court summed up the Indian political experience in America as follows: "These Indian tribes are wards of the nation. . . . They owe no allegiance to the States, and receive from them no protection. Because of the local ill feeling, the people of the States where they are found are often their deadliest enemies."[22]

Suffrage is almost entirely a state matter so far as determining the standards of voting eligibility. According to Article I, Section 4, of the Constitution, states shall prescribe the "times, places, and manner" of holding elections. Thus, the states are able to control by their own statutes whether Indians are permitted to exercise the franchise. The rationales presented by states to prevent Indians from registering to vote can be divided into four main categories: severance of tribal relations; "Indians not taxed"; guardianship; and residency.

Severance of Tribal Relations. Abandonment of traditional Indian culture was once a prerequisite for Indian citizenship and for participation in some state politics. The early Minnesota constitution

157

granted citizenship only to Indians who had "adopted the language, customs and habits of civilization."[23] South Dakota law also prohibited Indians from voting or holding office "while maintaining tribal relations."[24] The constitutions of Idaho and North Dakota contained similar language.[25] In addition to these state constitutions, the Supreme Court in *Elk* v. *Wilkins* cited 12 treaties, four statutes, four judicial decisions, and eight Attorney General opinions that required "proof of fitness for civilization" before Indians could obtain citizenship and vote.[26]

In *Swift* v. *Leach*,[27] a North Dakota court considered whether Indians were eligible to vote under Section 121 of the North Dakota constitution, which provided that qualified electors shall consist of "citizens of the United States" and "civilized persons of Indian descent who shall have severed their tribal relations." In ruling that the Indians were eligible to vote, the court heard numerous witnesses testify that the Indians lived "generally as white people live; that they have ceased to live in tribes; they do not owe obedience to chiefs; they have severed their tribal relations; that their progress, education, and ability to participate in governmental affairs compares favorably with the whites."[28]

"**Indians Not Taxed.**" The phrase "Indians not taxed" has been used frequently in state constitutions and statutes to exclude Indians from voting. The phrase originally appeared in the Constitution in Article 1, Section 2, which states that Indians not taxed shall not be counted as "free persons" in determining the representation of any state in Congress or in computing direct taxes to be levied by the United States.[29] The phrase reappears in Section 2 of the Fourteenth Amendment and in the Civil Rights Act of April 9, 1866,[30] declaring who shall be federal citizens. It also has been used to exclude Indians in the apportionment of representatives to a territorial or state legislature.[31]

The basic justification for states disallowing the vote to Indians is that those who do not pay taxes should not be permitted to vote. Furthermore, if a state government has no jurisdiction over the reservation on which Indians reside, then Indians should not be able to participate in the selection of state officials. This argument, however, goes to the heart of tribal sovereign immunity.

Typical of the view that Indians not taxed should not vote is the decision of the Minnesota Supreme Court in *Opsahl* v. *Johnson*,[32] which stated:

> It cannot for a moment be considered that the Framers of the Constitution intended to grant the right of suffrage to persons who were under no obligation to obey the laws enacted as a result of such grant. Or, in other words, that those who do not come within the operations of the laws of the state, nevertheless shall have the power to make and impose laws upon others. The idea is repugnant to our form of government. No one should participate in the making of laws which he need not obey.[33]

In 1940, five states—Idaho, Maine, Mississippi, New Mexico, and Washington—prohibited "Indians not taxed" from voting,[34] while granting the ballot to whites not taxed. On January 26, 1938, the Solicitor of the Department of the Interior issued an opinion concerning denial of the franchise to Indians. He concluded with the following observation:

> I am of the opinion that the Fifteenth Amendment clearly prohibits any denial of the right to vote to Indians under circumstances in which non-Indians would be permitted to vote. The laws of Idaho, New Mexico, and Washington which would exclude Indians not taxed from voting in effect exclude citizens of one race from voting on grounds which are not applied to citizens of other races. For this reason such laws are unconstitutional under the Fifteenth Amendment.[35]

Eventually four of the states permitted Indians to vote regardless of taxation, but New Mexico persisted in its efforts to disfranchise Indians based on taxation.

In 1948, an Indian named Miguel Trujillo from Isleta Pueblo in New Mexico was denied the right to vote because he did not pay state taxes on his property. Mr. Trujillo filed a suit in federal court challenging the phrase "Indians not taxed" contained in the New Mexico constitution.[36] The three-judge panel found that the prohibition in the New Mexico constitution amounted to a violation of the Fourteenth and Fifteenth Amendments. Judge Phillips stated, for the court:

> The New Mexico Constitution . . . says that 'Indians not taxed' may not vote, although they possess every other qualification. We are unable to escape the conclusion that, under the Fourteenth and Fifteenth Amendments, that constitutes a discrimination on the grounds of race. Any other citizen, regardless of race, in the State of New Mexico who has not paid one cent of tax of any kind or character, if he possesses the other qualifications, may vote. An Indian, and only an Indian, in order to meet the qualifications of a voter, must have paid a tax. How you can escape the conclusion that makes a requirement with respect to an Indian as a qualification to exercise the elective franchise and does not make that requirement with respect to the member of any race is beyond me. I just feel like the conclusion is inescapable.[37]

The cry of "representation without taxation" echoed again in the early 1970s in New Mexico and Arizona. In 1973 the Arizona Supreme Court held that an Indian may be elected to a county position even though he is immune from county and state taxation.[38] Similarly, the New Mexico Supreme Court ruled in 1975 that Indians may vote on a school board issue even though they are not taxed for repayment of a school bond.[39]

Guardianship. A third means employed by states to deny Indians the vote was to claim Indians were under guardianship and therefore ineligible to participate in the electorate. According to the

160

Arizona constitution, "No person under guardianship, *non compos mentis*, or insane shall be qualified to vote in any election."[40] In 1928 two Pima Indians attempted to register to vote in the first presidential election held after the 1924 Citizenship Act had granted them citizenship. Their registration request was denied because, according to the county registrar, the Indians were under guardianship of the federal government and therefore not residents of the state.

In *Porter* v. *Hall*,[41] the Arizona Supreme Court upheld the denial, using the following rationale:

> It is undisputed law, laid down by the Supreme Court of the United States innumerable times, from the famous case of *Cherokee Nation* v. *Georgia*, 5 Pet. 1, 8 L.Ed. 25, to the present time, that all Indians are wards of the federal government and as such are entitled to the care and protection due from a guardian to his ward.[42]

The court then concluded that Indians in Arizona were "within the meaning of our constitutional provision, 'persons under guardianship,' and not entitled to vote."[43]

For 20 years *Porter* v. *Hall* was allowed to stand unchallenged. But upon returning home after fighting in World War II, many Indian veterans insisted on the right to vote. This time, in *Harrison* v. *Laveen*,[44] the Arizona Supreme Court took a different view. The court distinguished between different types of guardianship. A judicially established guardianship was found to have no application to the federal status of Indians in Arizona as a class. The guardianship described in *Cherokee Nation* v. *Georgia* was designed to preserve the political and social well being of Indians, thus allowing Indians the right to vote in Arizona. *Porter* was expressly overruled by *Harrison*.

Residency. The final reason used by states to bar reservation Indians from the polls was the residence clause in certain election statutes. Just because a person is a citizen of a state does not mean he or she is a "resident." The New Mexico and Utah courts wrestled with the issue of whether a person living on a reservation within the territorial limits of a state was a resident. In 1962 the New Mexico Supreme Court declared that Indians living on reservations were in fact residents of the state.[45]

Utah, however, held the opposite view. In *Allen* v. *Merrell*,[46] the Utah court engaged in an elaborate discussion of the "separateness" of reservation Indians. The court reasoned that Indians had a separate culture, spoke a different language, and were unfamiliar with state government processes. It also noted that once Indians begin to accept state responsibilities, such as owning land and paying taxes, they may then qualify as residents and participate in state elections. The *Allen* case was appealed to the Supreme Court, which vacated the decision and remanded the case to Utah for rehearing.[47]

Prior to rehearing, however, the Utah state legislature repealed the statute barring Indians from voting based on residency. Utah was the last state to permit Indians to exercise their voting franchise.

Political Participation Today

Most of the blatant legislation prohibiting Indians from voting has been repealed or struck down by the courts. In addition to gaining the right to vote, court decisions have sustained the right of Indians to serve on state court juries,[48] hold state public offices,[49] and be counted in legislative apportionment.[50]

With the Voting Rights Act of 1965, Congress contributed to the expansion of voting rights for Indians. Numerous jurisdictions with large Indian populations are covered by the act's Section 5 preclearance requirements, and must submit any changes in their voting laws to the Department of Justice. Moreover, prior to the passage of the Voting Rights Act, literacy tests were used to disenfranchise Indians in Arizona. The act banned such tests.

One of the more difficult obstacles that Indians face when voting is the language barrier. In 1975, when the Voting Rights Act was renewed, it required bilingual voting information and ballots to assist non-English-speaking minorities. Indian voters have profited from this requirement.

162

Recent Litigation

In the past 25 years there has been a dramatic increase in Indian voting and candidacies in state and local governments. As a consequence, there has been an increase in voting rights legislation. In *Windy Boy* v. *County of Big Horn*,[51] Crow and Northern Cheyenne plaintiffs successfully challenged the county and school district's at-large election schemes as violative of Section 2 of the Voting Rights Act. Similar voting rights suits challenging at-large elections have been brought in South Dakota,[52] New Mexico,[53] North Carolina,[54] Arizona,[55] and Colorado.[56]

Other discriminatory election laws and practices have also been challenged. Many of these challenges occurred in South Dakota. As late as 1975, South Dakota effectively denied Indian residents the right to vote in certain county elections.[57] The Eighth Circuit held that denial of an Indian resident's right to run for a county commissioner office in South Dakota violated the equal protection clause.[58] In 1984 Indian voters there successfully challenged a county auditor's rejection of voter registration following an Indian registration drive.[59] In *Black Bull* v. *Dupree School District*,[60] the state's Indian voters challenged the denial of polling places in outlying Indian communities for school district elections. In 1986, a South Dakota county auditor was found to have violated the Voting Rights Act because the auditor refused to make available sufficient quantities of voter registration forms to Indian voters to enable them to mount a registration drive on the Indian reservation.[61]

In *Sanchez* v. *King*,[62] New Mexico's reapportionment plan was found to be violative of the one-person-one-vote principle; a court-imposed redistricting plan was ordered into effect to bring the state into compliance. Alaska Natives have also challenged the city of Anchorage's reapportionment plan.[63]

Getting Out the Vote

Despite the various impediments to voting, Indians have been going to the polls in significant numbers. However, there has been very little research on the impact of Indian voting.[64] There are a number of reasons for the paucity of data on Indian voting. First, many Indians live in remote areas of the country. Second, there are language and cultural barriers. Finally, Indians in the overall population comprise only a small percentage. A great deal of research still needs to be done on Indian voting. Increased interest in the outcome of Indian voting will probably induce increased levels of participation.

There are many influences on the Indian vote. It is safe to say that Indians vote for or against a candidate or a party because of the person's action on some Indian bill of vital importance to them.[65] For example, Indians in Idaho worked hard for Senator Frank Church and generally voted for him. The one exception was a tribe that voted for Herman Welker, who secured a bill important to their welfare.[66] The Indian vote also has made a difference in the elections of Senators George McGovern of South Dakota, Lee Metcalf of Montana, and Howard Cannon of Nevada.

Navajo voters maintain a high degree of loyalty to Democratic nominees for the Senate, primarily because of Republican support for a bill that was very unpopular among Navajos—the Steiger Land Settlement Bill partitioning the Navajo-Hopi Joint Use area. As a result, 88 percent of Navajos voted for Democratic senatorial candidate Dennis DeConcini when he ran against Sam Steiger in 1976.[67] Contrary to the Navajo position, the Hopi Tribe supported the Steiger bill. During the 1976 election, they rallied behind Steiger: He received 68 percent of the Hopi vote.[68]

There is also no doubt that Indians' participation in national and state elections has been low because of a lack of communication between candidates and party campaign committees with Indian communities about issues and candidates; ineffective organization on the part of Indians; and Indians' insufficient experience in the mechanics of registration and voting.

One of the most important factors in getting Indians to the polls has been the establishment and growth of organizations, both tribal and intertribal. These organizations have interpreted issues confronting Indians, disseminated information on candidates, and explained the mechanics of voting. Additionally, tribes have established their tribal elections to coincide with federal elections. This results in a much higher turnout for federal elections because more tribal members vote in tribal elections. Also, tribal voter education and registration projects have greatly increased Indian voting.

Registration drives are a common occurrence at chapter houses (i.e., tribal district meeting halls), district meetings, powwows, community dinners, and other tribal functions. A 1986 Indian political poll of tribal leaders showed that 65 percent of tribes or communities actively engage in voter registration efforts.[69]

Voter education is another key to increasing Indian participation. Many Indians are unaware of the need to register in order to vote in state elections. Some Indians mistakenly think that being on a tribal voting list makes them eligible to vote in state elections. Others do not realize they are required to vote at least every four years to remain registered. Confusion has been caused by overlapping tribal voting districts, county lines, voting precincts, school districts, and legislative districts. Many Indians who face language barriers would prefer the use of picture ballots rather than having only the names of candidates.[70]

A Growing Awareness

The questions of citizenship and blatant state barriers are largely moot. Thirty-two years ago, Utah—the last holdout among the states—repealed its law that had disfranchised Indian voters. Nevertheless, as in the case of other minorities, Indians will no doubt continue to face newly devised electoral mechanisms to perpetuate white political control.

There is, however, a growing awareness among Indians that they have the potential to influence policy as well as local and regional elections. Their increased level of voting is a manifestation of this awareness. The issues of water rights, natural resources, fishing, and jurisdiction play an important role in local, regional, and national politics. Indian tribes will be major actors in this political scene through voting and political participation.

Notes

1. See *Washington* v. *Fishing Vessel Association*, 443 U.S. 658, 675 (1979).

2. The Framers of the Constitution gave Congress the power to "regulate commerce with foreign nations, among the several states, and with the Indian Tribes." See Article 1, Section 2, of the U.S. Constitution. Additionally, in Article 6, Clause 2, the supremacy clause declares that all prior and future treaties are the supreme law of the land.

3. *Worcester* v. *Georgia*, 31 U.S. (6 Pet.) 515, 558 (1832).

4. *Cherokee Nation* v. *Georgia*, 30 U.S. (5 Pet.) 1 (1831).

5. The Kansas Indians, 72 U.S. (5 Wall.) 737 (1866); *United States* v. *Kagama*, 118 U.S. 375 (1886).

6. *Cherokee Nation* v. *Georgia*, 30 U.S. (5 Pet.) 1(1831); *Worcester* v. *Georgia*, 31 U.S. (6 Pet.) 515,558 (1832).

7. In 1871, Congress ended treaty making with Indian tribes. See the Appropriations Act of March 3, 1871, ch. 120, 16 Stat. 544, 566 (codified at 25 U.S.C. Section 71).

8. *McKay* v. *Campbell*, 16 Fed. Cas. 161 (D. Ore. 1871) (No. 8840).

9. In the early citizenship case of *Scott* v. *Sandford*, 60 U.S. (19 How.) 393 (1857) (Dred Scott), the Supreme Court held that a black person could not be made a citizen, as the term is used in the Constitution, by either a state or through naturalization. The Supreme Court also stated in dictum that Indians were not originally citizens in the constitutional sense but that, unlike the treatment accorded blacks, Congress had the power to naturalize Indians because Indians were aliens for that purpose. Thus, this decision effectively precluded Indians from registering to vote if they were unable to prove that they were born under the jurisdiction of the United States.

10. 112 U.S. 94 (1884).

11. 112 U.S. 101-103 (1884).

12. 112 U.S. 99-101 (1884). Section 2 of the Fourteenth Amendment changed the formula for apportionment of the House of Representatives to eliminate the slave fraction. However, the amendment retained the exclusion of "Indians not taxed." When Section 2 was codified in 8 U.S.C. Section 1 (1926), this exclusion was deleted. See also *United States* v. *Osborn*, 2 Fed. 58 (D.C. Ore. 1880). On the effect of tribal membership upon citizenship, see *Katzenmeyer* v. *United States*, 225 U.S. 501, 523 (7th Cir. 1915).

13. 169 U.S. 649, 693 (1898).

14. Prior to 1871, some early treaties granted citizenship options to Indians. Indians were required to make a choice: They either had to accept United States citizenship and receive an allotment, or retain tribal membership and move with their tribe to a new location. See, for example, "Treaty with the Cherokees," July 8, 1817, Article 8, 7 Stat. 156, 159; "Treaty with the Seneca and others," February 23, 1867, Articles 17, 18, and 19, 15 Stat. 513, 517-518.

15. Ch. 119, Section 6, 24 Stat. 388, 389 (codified as amended 25 U.S.C. Section 349).

16. Act of August 9, 1888, ch. 818, Section 2, 25 Stat. 392 (codified at 25 U.S.C. Section 182).

17. Act of March 3, 1873, ch. 332, Section 3, 17 Stat. 631 (Miami Tribal members).

18. Act of May 8, 1906, ch. 2348, 34 Stat. 182.

19. Op. Sol. I.D. [opinion of the Solicitor of the Department of Interior], M4018, July 29, 1921.

20. Act of November 6, 1919, ch. 95, 41 Stat. 350 (superseded in 1940).

21. Act of June 2, 1924, ch. 233, 43 Stat. 253.

22. *United States* v. *Kagama*, 118 U.S. 375 (1886).

23. See Article 7, Section 1, of the Minnesota constitution.

24. S.D. Codified Laws Ann., Section 92 (1929). This law remained on the books until 1951.

25. Article 6, Section 3, of the Idaho constitution (1890, repealed 1950); Section 121 of the North Dakota constitution (1889, repealed 1922).

26. *Elk* v. *Wilkins*, 112 U.S. 94, 100 (1884).

27. 45 N.D. 437, 178 N.W. 437 (1920).

28. 45 N.D. 437, 178 N.W. at 439 (1920).

29. Felix Cohen, *Handbook of Federal Indian Law*, 1942 ed. (Albuquerque: University of New Mexico Press), p. 156.

30. Section 1, 14 Stat. 27.

31. Act of June 19, 1878, 20 Stat. 178, 193.

32. 138 Minn. 42, 163 N.W. 988 (1917).

33. 138 Minn. 42, 163 N.W. 990 (1917).

34. Article 6, Section 3, of the Idaho constitution; Article 12, Section 1, of the New Mexico constitution; Article 6, Section 1, of the Washington constitution.

35. Op. Sol. I.D. (opinion of the Solicitor of the Department of Interior), M29596 (January 26, 1938).

36. *Trujillo* v. *Garley*, No. 1353, oral opinion (D.N.M. Aug. ll, 1948) (three-judge court).

37. *Trujillo* at 7-8.

38. *Shirley* v. *Superior Court*, 109 Ariz. 510, 513 P.2d 939 (1973), cert. denied, 415 U.S. 919 (1974).

39. *Prince* v. *Board of Education*, 88 N.M. 548, 543 P.2d 1176 (1975).

40. Article 8, Section 2, of the Arizona constitution.

41. 34 Ariz. 308, 271 P. 411 (1928).

42. Id. 34 Ariz. at 324-325, 271 P. at 417. In a strongly worded dissent, Chief Justice Ross pointed out that in *Cherokee Nation* v. *Georgia*, Justice John Marshall stated that the Indian's "relation to the United States resembles that of a ward to a guardian. . . ." In contrast to this statement, the Arizona constitution referred to an actual legal guardianship (271 P. at 419).

43. Id. 34 Ariz. at 332, 271 P. at 418.

44. 67 Ariz. 337, 196 P.2d 456 (1948).

45. *Montoya* v. *Bolack*, 70 N.M. 196, 372 P.2d 387 (1962). The Indian right to vote was vainly challenged by the unsuccessful candidate for lieutenant governor of New Mexico, who would have been the victor by 63 votes out of 300,000 cast if the Indian votes had been thrown out. He contended that since the state had no jurisdiction over the reservation, the polling places should not have been allowed thereon because of the difficulties that might have arisen in the event a violation of the New Mexico Election Code had occurred on the reservation.

46. 6 Utah 2d 32, 305 P.2d 490 (1956).

47. 353 U.S. 932 (1957).

48. *Dennison* v. *State of Arizona*, 34 Ariz. 144, 268 P. 617 (1928).

49. *Shirley* v. *Superior Court*, 109 Ariz. 510, 513 P.2d 939 (1973), cert. denied, 415 U.S. 919 (1974). See *Yamito* v. *Barber*, 348 F.Supp. 587 (D. Utah 1972) (three-judge court); Indian Oasis School District No. 40 v. Zambrano, 22 Ariz. App. 201, 526 P.2d 408 (1974).

50. *Goodluck* v. *Apache County*, 417 F. Supp. 13 (D. Ariz. 1975) (three-judge court), affirmed, 429 U.S. 876 (1976). See *Ely* v. *Klahr*, 403 U.S. 108, 118-119 (1971) (J. Douglas concurring) on remand, *Klahr* v. *Williams*, 339 F. Supp. 922, 926-28 (D. Ariz. 1972) (three-judge court).

51. 647 F. Supp. 1002 (D. Mont. 1986).

52. *Buckanaga* v. *Sisseton School District*, No. 84-1025 (D.S.D. 1985) (memorandum opinion), reversed and remanded, 804 F.2d 469 (8th Cir. 1986).

53. *Tso* v. *Cuba Independent School District*, No. 86-1023-JB (May 18, 1987) (consent decree); *Bowannie et al.* v. *Bernalillo School District*, No. Civ. 88-0121 JT, filed February 1988 (D.N.M. 1988); *Largo* v. *McKinley Consol. School District*, No. 84-1751 HB (Nov. 26, 1984); *Estevan* v. *Grants-Cibola County School District*, No. 84-1752 HB (Nov. 26, 1984); *Casuse* v. *City of Gallup*, No. 88-1007 HB (D.N.M. 1988).

54. *Love* v. *Lumberton City Board of Education*, No. 87-105-CIV-3 (D.N.C. 1987).

55. *Clark* v. *Holbrook Public School District No. 3*, No. 88-0148 PCT RGS (D. Ariz. 1988).

56. *Cuthair* v. *Montezuma-Cortez*, Colorado School District, No. RE-1, No. 89-C-964 (D. Colo. 1990) (consent decree).

57. *Little Thunder* v. *South Dakota*, 518 F.2d 1253 (8th Cir. 1975).

58. *United States* v. *South Dakota*, 636 F.2d 241 (8th Cir.

1980).

59. *American Horse* v. *Kundert*, Civ. 84-5159 (D.S.D. Nov. 5, 1984).

60. Civ. 86-3012 (D.S.D. May 16, 1986).

61. *Fiddler* v. *Sisker*, Civ. No. 86-3050 (D.S.D. Oct. 24, 1986).

62. 550 F. Supp. 13 (D.N.M. 1982), affirmed, 459 U.S. 801 (1983).

63. *Ratcliff* v. *Municipality of Anchorage*, No. A86-036 (D. Alaska 1989).

64. Helen L. Peterson, "American Indian Political Participation," in *Annals of the American Academy of Political and Social Science*, vol. 311 (May 1957); Jack E. Holmes, *Politics in New Mexico* (Albuquerque: University of New Mexico Press, 1967); Stephen J. Kunitz and Jerrold E. Levy, "Navajo Voting Patterns," in *Plateau*, vol. 43, no.1 (Summer 1970); Leonard G. Ritt, "Empirical Approaches to the Study of American Indian Political Behavior," paper delivered April 2-5, 1980.

65. A recent political behavior study at the Tohono O'Odham and Gila River Reservations in Arizona concluded that a candidate's stand on Indian issues and concern for Indian people were very important, receiving high percentages of 81 percent and 86 percent, respectively. See the *National Indian Youth Council*, "Political and Attitudes Behavior Poll at Tohono O'Odham and Gila River, Arizona" (Albuquerque, 1986). A poll conducted on the Navajo Reservation showed that 69 percent of Navajos found most important a candidate's concern for Indian issues and people. See the *National Indian Youth Council*'s "Navajo Indian Political Attitudes and

Behavior Poll" (Albuquerque, October 1984), p. 16.

66. Peterson, "American Indian Political Participation," in *Annals of the American Academy of Political and Social Science*, vol. 311 (May 1957), p. 125.

67. Daniel McCool, "Indian Voting," in *American Indian Policy in the Twentieth Century* (Norman: Oklahoma University Press, 1985), pp. 123-124.

68. *Ibid.*

69. The *National Indian Youth Council*, "National American Indian Political and Issues Poll" (Albuquerque, 1986).

70. The *National Indian Youth Council*, "Navajo Indian Political Attitudes and Behavior Poll" (Albuquerque, October 1984), p. 28.

Many naturalized citizens come from countries where participation in a democratic process is not the "norm." In fact, to participate politically is to place oneself at personal risk.

In Pursuit of Political Equality

Henry Der

The U.S. Congress approved the 1975 bilingual election amendments to the Voting Rights Act of 1965 to promote the political enfranchisement of hundreds of thousands of language minority citizens in America.[1]

As President Gerald R. Ford signed these amendments into law, Chinese for Affirmative Action (CAA)[2] had high hopes that political equality would become a reality for thousands of Chinese-speaking citizens with limited English proficiency who had been excluded historically from the democratic process because of the English language barrier and other institutional electoral practices.

But before the ink even dried, opponents of bilingual elections and local election officials themselves launched attacks against the voting rights of these language minority citizens. In fact, to this day, the goals of the 1975 bilingual election amendments have not been fulfilled, nor have Chinese American citizens in San Francisco achieved political equality.

Asian Americans and the Vote

Asian Americans are the fastest growing minority group in America today.[3] More than one-third of all Asian Americans in our country live in California.[4]

In the continental United States, San Francisco is home to the largest concentration of Asian Americans among major American cities. According to population estimates based on the 1980 U.S.

Census, close to 30 percent of all San Franciscans are Asian Americans.[5]

Among the diverse Asian American racial groups (Japanese, Filipino, Koreans, Vietnamese), Chinese Americans constitute the largest Asian group, approximately 16 percent of the city's population.[6] There are 31,000 registered Chinese American voters in San Francisco,[7] approximately eight percent of all registered voters.[8]

Yet only one-third of all Chinese Americans in San Francisco are registered to vote. Another one-third of Chinese Americans are eligible to register to vote but have not done so. (The remaining one-third are ineligible because of their permanent resident alien status.)

The overall voter registration rate of all qualified San Francisco residents is 60 percent.[9] The Chinese American voter registration rate is only one-half of the overall rate for all San Franciscans.

The Adverse Impact of Low Voter Turnout

The low Chinese American voter registration rate in San Francisco has hurt the level of Chinese American representation in all aspects of city government. No Chinese American or Asian American has ever been elected to the San Francisco Board of Supervisors in citywide, at-large elections.[10] In the entire history of city government, only one Chinese American has ever been selected to head one of the 42 major city departments.[11]

Among 18 major city departments where Asian American professionals or technicians have either met or exceeded work force parity, Asian Americans are visibly absent from administrative and managerial positions.[12] The historic and ongoing exclusion of Chinese Americans from top-level leadership positions in city government reflects the lack of political equality and recognition of Chinese Americans.

In the San Francisco public school system, the representation of Chinese Americans and other Asian Americans in line-administrative positions is no better. There are no Chinese Americans in positions that could lead to possible appointment as superintendent of the San

Francisco Unified School District or of another school district—this despite the fact that Chinese American students constitute the single largest ethnic group in the school district's total student population, 22 percent.[13]

In 1982 the San Francisco Community College Board of Governors, comprising a majority of racial minorities, appointed Mr. Hilary Hsu as chancellor/superintendent. Hsu became the first Chinese American to lead a major postsecondary educational institution in the Bay Area. His tenure was marred, though, by considerable racial hostility and resistance toward his leadership. Throughout Hsu's administration, the predominantly white faculty of City College of San Francisco challenged and attacked numerous appointments and administrative decisions he made. Relations between the City College faculty and Hsu deteriorated so much that in 1988 the faculty in an unprecedented move asked a visiting accreditation team not to grant accreditation to the institution.

Attempts to Rectify Historic Wrongs

The disregard for Chinese American concerns and interests in San Francisco is related directly to historic attitudes about the Chinese American community and the lack of fulfillment of the goals of the bilingual election amendments to the Voting Rights Act. Consequently, CAA has had to initiate legal and administrative actions to ensure that local election officials comply with federal and state voting rights laws and to encourage Chinese Americans to believe they have rights within the democratic process.

Immediately after the 1975 amendments became law, CAA persuaded the San Francisco Board of Supervisors to establish a Multilingual Citizens Task Force to help implement the Voting Rights Act. In spite of the appointment of concerned language minority citizens to the task force, Thomas Kearney, the San Francisco Registrar of Voters, took administrative actions that led to the demise of the task force within one year of its creation.

Prior to the June 1976 primary election, CAA communicated to

177

Kearney that, based on the number of requests for election materials in Chinese and on census population data, at least 47 precincts out of more than 900 in San Francisco should be assigned a Chinese bilingual poll worker to render bilingual oral assistance. Monitoring the 47 precincts on election day, CAA found that only 14 of these targeted precincts—or 29.8 percent—had a Chinese bilingual poll worker. Further, CAA pointed out to Kearney that of the six officially designated voter registration sites throughout the city, none were located in either of the two affected language minority communities—Chinese and Hispanic.

During the 1977 San Francisco municipal election, CAA informed Kearney as to which San Francisco precincts needed bilingual poll assistance. For the June 1978 primary election, CAA indicated to Kearney that 61 precincts would need bilingual poll assistance.[14] As in previous election years, Kearney essentially ignored CAA's communications with him regarding the necessity of targeting Chinese bilingual precincts.

CAA and other community groups had no alternative but to approach the U.S. Attorney and the U.S. Department of Justice to enforce Section 203 of the Voting Rights Act in San Francisco.[15] Prior to the June 1978 primary election, U.S. Attorney General G. William Hunter informed Kearney of his obligation to comply with federal law. After several on-site visits by Justice Department officials, the U.S. Attorney notified the registrar that there were no Chinese-speaking election officials assigned to several precincts in the Chinese community where a clear need for such assistance had been demonstrated, and that in still other precincts more assistance than had been provided was required to meet the needs of those precincts.

Federal and Community Observers at the Polls

On June 6, 1978, teams of assistant attorneys and law clerks from the Office of the U.S. Attorney as well as bilingual community volunteers observed targeted bilingual precincts in the Chinese community. Of the 48 Chinese precincts observed that day, only 29 had a bilingual poll worker. Voter confusion or hesitancy to proceed with the electoral process by language minority voters was noted as commonplace in the Chinese precincts.[16]

Other deficiencies observed by these teams of federal and community observers included ineffective assistance rendered by bilingual officials at the polls due to lack of adequate training. In some precincts the presence of one bilingual poll official was insufficient to handle all the voters who could not speak English. Oftentimes the use of the voting machine was explained by the English-speaking poll officials. Further, many language minority voters were automatically given the English ballot without being asked whether they needed a minority language ballot.

Between the June 1978 primary election and the November 1978 general election, Registrar Kearney had enough time to demonstrate how he would better comply with federal law. Because he still made little effort to comply, the U.S. Attorney filed a lawsuit in the federal court for the Northern District of California in October 1978 to seek compliance.[17] Federal court judge Cecil Poole then issued a temporary order requiring the registrar to implement the following actions for the November 1978 general election: (1) secure the assistance of the California Secretary of State to target Chinese and Hispanic bilingual precincts; (2) secure the assistance of community groups to recruit bilingual poll officials; (3) conduct training sessions for bilingual poll officials, particularly in cooperation with community groups; (4) notify all poll officials in targeted precincts of their obligation to assist non-English-speaking voters; and (5) post bilingual signs notifying voters about the availability of bilingual poll assistance. A federal examiner was also appointed to monitor all polling activities on election day.

With the cooperation of community groups, an almost sufficient number of bilingual poll workers were recruited within three days to cover the targeted bilingual precincts on election day.

Continued Defiance of Federal Law

While the U.S. Attorney was attempting to negotiate a settlement with the City Attorney's Office over the lawsuit, Registrar Kearney was given all of 1979 to demonstrate what he could do on his own to comply with the requirements of federal law. For the November 1979 municipal election, however, he again demonstrated his defiance of federal law by not recruiting a sufficient number of bilingual poll officials. By then, the number of targeted Chinese bilingual precincts had reached 69, yet only 36 of these 69 precincts had bilingual poll workers assigned.

Hauled into federal court immediately after the November 1979 municipal election to explain his failure to recruit an adequate number of bilingual poll officials, Registrar Kearney revealed, when questioned about his personal feelings about the 1975 amendments:

> "My feelings about the necessity for polling place workers, my personal feelings aside from the law is that it's not as necessary as a lot of people think. However, that doesn't influence my efforts in trying to comply with the law."[18]

Further questioning of Kearney by Assistant U.S. Attorney Amanda Metcalf revealed that he had made racial slurs against Chinese Americans during the preceding November 1978 general election when he got angry at his assistant for assigning a trainer to go to Chinatown, at the request of CAA, to train bilingual poll workers recruited by community groups:

> Assistant U.S. Attorney: "Mr. Kearney, did you state in the presence of Mr. Lamar Johnson (trainer), having been informed that he was going to the Chinese community to conduct training sessions for Chinese bilingual poll workers, did you state to him, quote, 'I don't want Lamar teaching those damn chinks' and also 'Damn chinks, they shouldn't get something special.'"

Mr. Kearney: "I may have said that. I don't know the exact text of that."

Later, under questioning by the federal court judge, Kearney admitted:

".... asked that we send an instructor to a location in Chinatown to conduct a class for Chinese polling place workers only. And I thought that wasn't necessary. And knowing that I felt that way, one of our staff scheduled Mr. Johnson to conduct a class in Chinatown against my wishes and I became angry and said something approximately like what was quoted.... I can't deny that I said it."

It became evident from this court testimony that the registrar's personal feelings about bilingual elections did interfere with his efforts to comply with the 1975 amendments. The Chinese American community succeeded in persuading Chief Administrative Officer Roger Boas to remove Kearney from his position as Registrar of Voters.[19] After Kearney's removal, the city made remarkable improvements to comply with federal law.

A Promise Abandoned

More importantly, on May 19, 1980, the U.S. Department of Justice and the City and County of San Francisco entered into a comprehensive consent decree to take the following actions:

1. Develop and implement a recruitment program for bilingual poll officials to commence four months prior to every election;

2. Establish effective procedures to target precincts in need of bilingual poll workers;

3. Provide appropriate training and written materials to all bilingual poll workers;

4. Establish an election day "hotline" for non-English-speaking voters;

181

5. Train all poll officials regarding the manner in which they are to assist language minority voters who vote in nondesignated Chinese language precincts;

6. Develop a glossary of commonly used election terms in Chinese;

7. Assign at least two bilingual poll officials to those precincts where it is determined that there are at least 25 percent or more Chinese-speaking voters;

8. Develop a voter registration outreach plan to actively seek out and register language minority citizens;

9. Establish effective procedures for distribution of bilingual voting and registration materials;

10. Initiate contact and work with community groups to identify and secure sites for voter registration;

11. Identify and maintain a listing of underregistered Chinese-speaking precincts.[20]

But Chinese-speaking citizens never had the opportunity to reap the full benefits of this consent decree. Shortly after it was signed and implementation was begun, instead of becoming the beneficiaries of voting rights protection, Chinese American citizens—along with Hispanic American citizens—became the victims of vicious, unrelenting attacks by the opponents of bilingual elections.

A Bilingual Voter Witch-Hunt

In April 1982 CAA learned through a local news reporter about a probe launched by the newly appointed U.S. Attorney for the Northern District of California to investigate the citizenship of foreign-born voters requesting bilingual ballots in nine San Francisco Bay Area counties: San Mateo, Santa Clara, Alameda, Napa, Sonoma, Santa Cruz, Monterey, Contra Costa, and San Francisco.

In a letter dated April 19, 1982, addressed to the district attorney of each of these nine counties, U.S. Attorney Joseph Russoniello cited a February 1981 Santa Clara County District Attorney investigation, prompted by the results of a Santa Clara County

Registrar of Voters Office survey of 100 newly registered persons of foreign birth. This survey preliminarily found that of the 100 registered voters sampled, 20 were not U.S. citizens and 11 could not be located.

Without revealing the unreliability of this survey by the Santa Clara Registrar of Voters Office, Russoniello warned in his letter to Bay Area district attorneys:

> We are concerned, as I am sure you are, that if as many as 30 percent of the newly-registered foreign born persons vote even though they are not eligible to do so, especially given the expected intensive effort to register non-English speaking persons, the elections to be held June 8 [1982] may be so affected that the results are subject to court challenge.

Under the guise of protecting the integrity of the June 1982 primary election and the right to vote by "bona fide" English-speaking citizens already registered to vote, Russoniello requested that each district attorney:

> Submit by April 30, 1982, at random the names and dates of birth of 25 persons of new registration, whose affidavits of registration reflect (1) a foreign country as place of birth and (2) a preference for election materials in a language other than English.

Russoniello then informed these district attorneys that the lists of 25 names from each county would be forwarded to the Immigration and Naturalization Service for verification of status.

Upon learning of Russoniello's witch-hunt against voters who did not speak English, several groups and concerned individuals—among them CAA, the Hispanic Coalition for Human Rights, the San Francisco Latino Voter Registration Education Project, and language-minority citizens—launched a massive community protest against this secret probe. On May 7, 1982, these groups and individuals filed a lawsuit in federal court for the

Northern District of California to enjoin Russoniello from proceeding with the probe.[21]

Even though these plaintiffs did not succeed in securing a court-ordered injunction to halt this bilingual voter probe, Russoniello failed to uncover any illegal voter registration by ineligible individuals. Although he claimed that the lawsuit prevented him from continuing his probe, his witch-hunt had the net effect of adversely disrupting voter registration drives in language minority communities in the San Francisco Bay Area. Individuals who were potential registered voters expressed concern to civil rights groups that they might be unduly harassed if they were to register to vote.

In response to this secret bilingual voter probe, the California State Assembly Committee on Elections and Reapportionment held a public hearing in San Francisco on May 21, 1982, to solicit testimony about the effects of the Russoniello witch-hunt. Based on the public testimony presented, in September 1982 the California State Legislature enacted AB 2949, authored by Assemblyman Richard Alatorre of Los Angeles, to protect bilingual voter registration rolls by requiring the issuance of a court subpoena before the identity of bilingual voters is revealed.

The Power of Anti-Bilingual Forces

After the 1982 voter probe, antibilingual election forces in California gathered sufficient numbers of signatures of registered voters to place a series of local and state initiatives on the ballot calling for the repeal of the bilingual election provisions of the Voting Rights Act. While these initiatives were largely advisory in nature, nonregistered Chinese- and Spanish-speaking citizens received the "unwelcome" message loud and clear.

In November 1983, by a vote of 70 percent to 30 percent, San Francisco voters approved Proposition O calling on the U.S. Congress to repeal the bilingual election provisions of the Voting Rights Act.

In 1984, by a similarly wide margin, the voters of California approved Proposition 38, which called on the state legislature to

184

write to Congress to repeal the 1975 amendments to the Voting Rights Act. The amendments benefit non-English-speaking citizens. Pointing out the "divisive" nature of bilingual ballots, in 1986 the English-only movement in California qualified Proposition 63 for the November general election. The proposition declared English the official language of the State of California. Again California voters approved this state proposition overwhelmingly. In light of its passage, numerous Chinese-speaking citizens assumed that bilingual ballots would no longer be available or that bilingual poll assistance would not be provided.

Factors That Hinder Voting

A 1987 study of Chinese American voter registration conducted by the Fellows of Coro Foundation[22] indicated that among Chinese American citizens eligible to register to vote, those who were foreign born, of low income, less educated, women, young adults aged 18 to 30, and unable to speak English were least likely to be registered to vote.

In addition to citing apathy among these potential registered voters, this 1987 study found that among unregistered Chinese American citizens, lack of information on how to register and lack of information in the Chinese language were barriers to voter registration.

Given the low Chinese American voter registration rate and voter participation, Chinese community groups and individuals cooperated in 1975 to form the Chinese American Voters Education Committee (CAVEC) to promote voter registration and to encourage voter participation. CAVEC raises private funds each year from the community to conduct street corner and door-to-door voter registration drives.[23]

Even though voter registration by mail is permitted in California, personal experiences and studies indicate that "high touch/high personal contact" is needed to persuade and assist Chinese American citizens to register to vote, particularly for the non-English-speaking or foreign born. Many naturalized citizens come from countries where participation in a democratic process is not the "norm." In fact, to participate politically is to place oneself at personal risk.

Strategies for Increasing Voter Participation

Both short- and long-range strategies are needed to enhance voter registration. Short-range strategies include the continuous use of street-corner voter registration tables and door-to-door contact. Long-range strategies include outreach to high schools with a substantial foreign-born Chinese student population, in-depth discussion and understanding of the day-to-day political dynamics of local government in community college and adult education classes, and identification of Chinese American political candidates to encourage interest in and access to political institutions among non-English-speaking citizens.

In spite of the numerous administrative setbacks suffered by Chinese American voters in San Francisco, the bilingual election provisions of the Voting Rights Act have enabled many non-English-speaking Chinese American voters to participate in the political process. While bilingual election materials alone are not sufficient to guarantee full voter participation among language minorities,[24] bilingual written and oral assistance has opened the doors of democracy to many citizens who would otherwise have been shut out because of the English language barrier.

The bilingual election provisions of the Voting Rights Act have weathered many attacks. In the process, they have evolved into a durable foundation of voter participation for language minority voters.

Notes

1. As amended in 1982, Section 203 of the Voting Rights Act of 1965 provides:

> The Congress finds that, through the use of various practices and procedures, citizens of language minorities have been effectively excluded from participation in the electoral process. Among other factors, the denial of the right to vote of such minority group citizens is ordinarily directly related to the unequal educational opportunities afforded them, resulting in high illiteracy and low voting participation. . . .
>
> Prior to August 6, 1992, no State or political subdivision shall provide registration or voting notices, forms, instructions, assistance, or other materials or information relating to the electoral process, including ballots, only in the English language if the Director of the Census determines (i) that more than 5 percent of the citizens of voting age of such State or political subdivision are members of a single language minority and (ii) that the illiteracy rate of such persons as a group is higher than the national illiteracy rate. . . .for the purposes of this subsection, illiteracy means the failure to complete the fifth primary grade.

2. Founded in 1969, CAA is a voluntary membership-supported organization dedicated to defending and promoting equality and justice for Chinese Americans. With the cooperation of KPIX-TV and the San Francisco Community College District, in 1970 CAA created the 65 half-hour "Practical English TV" series and accompanying four-volume Practical English Handbooks to enable Chinese adults with limited English proficiency to learn the language in their homes.

3. According to the U.S. Bureau of the Census's "A Profile of the Asian Pacific Islander Population, 1990," the Asian American population grew 107 percent between 1980 and 1990.

4. According to the Census Bureau's "A Profile of the Asian Pacific Islander Population, 1990," two of every five Asian Americans in the United States live in California.

5. According to the 1990 U.S. Census, 28 percent of all San Franciscans are Asian Americans.

6. Comprising 18 percent of the city's total population, Chinese Americans continue to constitute the largest Asian group in San Francisco, according to the 1990 U.S. Census.

7. Henry Louie, chairperson of the Chinese American Voters Education Committee, estimates that as of 1992 there are 37,000 registered Chinese American voters in San Francisco. Louie's nonprofit organization was established to promote voter registration among Chinese Americans.

8. According to the Office of the San Francisco Registrar of Voters, there were 432,867 registered voters as of May 10, 1992. Using Henry Louie's estimate of 37,000 registered Chinese American voters currently residing in San Francisco (see note 7), one finds that in 1992 approximately 8.5 percent of all registered voters in San Francisco are Chinese American.

9. The overall voter registration rate of all qualified San Francisco residents has climbed to 88.5 percent, according to California Secretary of State March Fong Eu's Report of Registration. This report was published in Sacramento, California, on April 12, 1992.

10. San Francisco is both a city and county. It should be noted that as of 1992, only one Chinese American has been elected to the San Francisco Board of Supervisors in a citywide, at-large election.

11. As of early 1992, only two Chinese Americans have ever been selected to head one of San Francisco's 42 major city departments: Jeffrey Lee, former director of the San Francisco Department of Public Works; and Ed Lee, director of the San Francisco Human Rights Commission.

When Jeffrey Lee was appointed director in 1979, Chief Administrative Officer Roger Boas initially had such great doubts about Lee's administrative abilities that two aides were also appointed to shore up this "perceived" weak Chinese American engineer-turned-administrator. Upon his retirement in 1985, Mr. Lee was hailed by many City Hall sources as an outstanding administrator who had led the city successfully through many difficult capital projects.

12. See Chinese for Affirmative Action's *The Broken Ladder: Asian Americans in City Government*, (San Francisco: CAA, 1989).

13. Chinese American students remain the largest ethnic group in the San Francisco School District's total student population, numbering 25 percent. See *San Francisco Unified School District Affirmative Action Report* (September 1991).

It is also worth noting that, according to this report, Asian American students—Chinese, Filipino, Vietnamese, Japanese, Korean, and others—now represent more than 45 percent of the total public school population in San Francisco.

14. See letters dated April 27 and May 26, 1978, to San Francisco Registrar of Voters Thomas Kearney from Chinese for Affirmative Action.

15. See note 1 for specific provisions of Section 203 of the Voting Rights Act.

16. See "Language Trouble at Poll" in the *San Francisco Chronicle* (June 7, 1978); "It's Not My Fault" and "City's Voteless Citizens Barred by Language" in the *San Francisco Examiner* (June 7, 1978); and CAA notes of community observers Susan Tam, Gloria Louie, Russell Lowe, Citania Tam, and Diana Hong.

17. See *U.S.A.* v. *City and County of San Francisco*, C-78 2521 CFP.

18. Court transcripts in *U.S.A.* v. *City and County of San Francisco*, C-78 2521 (November 1979).

19. Kearney was reassigned to work in the Sewer Department under San Francisco Department of Public Works director Jeffrey Lee.

20. See *U.S.A.* v. *City and County of San Francisco*, Consent Decree (three-judge court, May 19, 1980), signed by Judges Cecil F. Poole, Robert F. Peckham, and William H. Orrick.

21. See *Jose J. Olagues et al.* v. *Joseph P. Russoniello*, C 82 2102 SW.

22. Founded in 1942, the Coro Foundation is a nonprofit organization dedicated to providing leadership training to concerned community citizens.

23. For the November 1991 San Francisco municipal election, CAVEC registered close to 5,000 new Chinese American voters. See *CAVEC News* (CAVEC, January 1992).

24. Are bilingual election materials effective? Different community organizations, including the Asian American Legal Defense and Education Fund in New York and the Asian Pacific Legal Center of Southern California in Los Angeles, have conducted surveys to assess whether bilingual voting materials would be helpful to Asian American non-English-speaking citizens. See *Voter Rights Survey* (1991) by Jill M. Medina of the Asian Pacific Legal Center of Southern California.

In January 1992, with the support of the Chinese American Voters Education Committee (CAVEC), CAA conducted a telephone survey of 292 randomly selected, registered Chinese voters who have indicated a need for bilingual materials, out of a total of 6,284 registered non-English-speaking Chinese voters in San Francisco. The CAA survey found that 53 percent of respondents participated in the November 1991 San Francisco mayoral election. The voter participation rate of these non-English-speaking Chinese voters equaled that of all registered San Francisco voters in this election.

Among the 292 non-English-speaking Chinese voters in the survey, CAA also randomly selected 29 respondents to participate in focus group discussions to ascertain their voting behaviors and attitudes. Preliminary findings of this survey indicate the following:

• An overwhelming majority of the respondents read Chinese-language newspapers on a daily basis. They demonstrate an interest in news and current affairs.

• Most of the respondents watch television at least three hours a day; a little less than half of the respondents listen to the radio two and one-half hours a day.

• More than 90 percent heard about the November 1991 San Francisco mayoral candidates on television, with a similar percentage for the newspapers.

• Close to 100 percent saw or heard something about the mayoral candidates on a handbill, poster, or some other type of printed political advertisement.

• A substantial majority voted for the Chinese American

candidate in the November 1991 mayoral election.

• Close to 90 percent of the focus group respondents felt it very important or somewhat important that the availability of bilingual election materials encouraged them to vote in the November 1991 election.

• More than 90 percent of these respondents found the bilingual election materials very helpful or somewhat helpful.

• One hundred percent had no difficulty filling out the bilingual ballot.

• Close to one-third requested bilingual poll assistance on election day.

• Of 22 issues that may be of importance to their community, these focus group respondents ranked job security/employment, health care/health insurance, money, family, and law/order as the five most important issues. AIDS, homeland politics, difficulty in getting information on daily living, difficulty with American agencies, and lack of ethnic/community support groups were identified as the five least important issues.

These preliminary results indicate that non-English-speaking Chinese American voters follow news and current events, are aware of the political candidates, express a strong preference for ethnic political representation, share the same concerns about the economic and safety conditions of society as their English-speaking counterparts, and find bilingual voting materials very helpful and important.

Despite the barrier that language poses, non-English-speaking voters are citizens aware of and concerned about the political and social conditions affecting their lives. Clearly, absent bilingual voting materials, these citizens would not be able to cast an effective ballot or voice their political preference.

*It is true that many poor people don't
see a relationship between their vote and a
change in their own lives. And for good reason.
They are focused on survival this afternoon,
tomorrow, next week. Yet the political process
bears fruit—if at all—only after long delay.*

Bringing Voting to the People

Al Raby

The United States is facing an epidemic of nonparticipation in the political process. This apathy saps the strength of our democracy and tragically distorts national policy. For our democracy to survive and thrive, we need to bring more people, particularly low- and moderate-income people, into the democratic process.

The Importance of Voter Registration

Nothing sums up the urgency of registering more voters better than a few facts:

- In just three months in 1984, local Project VOTE! coalitions registered 528,851 people.[1] Keep these half-million voters in mind as you read the following points.

- In each of the three non-incumbent presidential races we have had from 1952 through 1988, a shift of 87,000 votes or less would have changed the outcome.[2] In 1960 a shift of 27,000 votes would have elected Richard Nixon instead of John Kennedy. In 1968 a shift of 87,000 votes would have elected Hubert Humphrey instead of Richard Nixon. And in 1976 a shift of 9,000 votes in Ohio and Hawaii would have elected Gerald Ford instead of Jimmy Carter.

• In 1980 a shift of 45,000 votes could have changed the outcome of six Senate races or twenty House races.

• In 1986 a shift of just 64,000 votes could have changed the results in nine U.S. Senate races.

In my own state of Illinois I've learned the truth of the old saying that every vote counts. In 1983, when I managed Harold Washington's campaign for mayor of Chicago, a shift of 17,944 votes would have defeated him in the primary, and a shift of 24,126 votes would have defeated him in the general election.

In 1984, Paul Simon of Illinois won election to the Senate by 89,000 votes after Project VOTE! coalitions registered 131,000 voters in the state. Although our work is nonpartisan, Simon says he would not have made it to the Senate had we not been there.

In fact, there have now been four Senate races, four House races, and 18 state and local races in which the number of voters that Project VOTE! coalitions have registered and turned out has exceeded the winning margin.[3] That's not to say we elected those senators; there were others who played roles as important or more important than ours. And besides, the real credit goes to hundreds of national and local groups and to the thousands of volunteers who make the work happen.

So the point is not to brag about Project VOTE! but to say that the efforts we all make to register voters—the efforts of the National Coalition on Black Voter Participation, the Southwest Voter Registration Education Project, the Churches Committee on Voter Registration, HumanServe, Disabled Voters, local Urban Leagues and NAACP chapters, sororities and fraternities, and so on—are terribly important. We must continue working at it and doing it even more effectively.

How much difference does all of this make? Just look at the Bork nomination, which the Leadership Conference on Civil Rights, among others, did so much to defeat. If just those four Senate races had come out differently, the Senate would now have a Republican majority, Strom Thurmond would have chaired the Bork hearings, and Bork would have been confirmed. A shift of a few votes in the Senate or House often means a shift of billions of dollars for programs we care about. And the impact often goes beyond money.

The History of Project VOTE!

Project VOTE! is the brainchild of Sandy Newman, which, I suppose, makes it a grandchild of the Leadership Conference on Civil Rights, since Newman started his civil rights career as a thirteen-year-old volunteer for the Leadership Conference under the tutelage of Clarence Mitchell, Joe Rauh, and Arnie Aronson.[4]

In 1981, cuts in food stamps and other social programs were sailing through Congress. Now, food stamps alone serve 22 million people, and the combined constituency of the social service programs that were being cut was roughly the size of Social Security. Yet Congress barely batted an eye as it slashed nearly all programs serving the poor. The reason was obvious: Poor people didn't vote.

Newman started Project VOTE! to pioneer the strategy of registering voters in welfare offices, food stamp, unemployment, and cheese lines—all the places where the poor are made to wait to receive "services" from an uncaring economy and government.

Project VOTE! focuses on increasing voter participation by low-income and minority voters in selected areas across the country. It registers voters, provides voter education, and works to strengthen the capabilities of local groups and organizers.

Project VOTE! coalitions have now registered more than 800,000 voters; provided voter education to these registrants and hundreds of thousands of additional citizens; and won sweeping changes in Illinois voter registration laws, making it possible for volunteers to register voters.[5] It also has filed 12 lawsuits, mostly against states and governors to protect the right to vote, and has won them all.

Myths About Voter Registration

Permit me to discuss some persistent myths about voter registration.

Myth #1: The poor are "too expensive" to register.

Yes, there are reasons why poor people are less likely than others to be registered. Often, registration barriers stand in the way. And it is true that many poor people don't see a relationship between their vote and a change in their own lives. And for good reason. They are focused on survival this afternoon, tomorrow, next week. Yet the political process bears fruit—if at all—only after long delay.

If one sits behind a card table in a shopping mall, the outsiders of our society will not come forward to sign up. But if we go aggressively to where they are, if we help them understand the connection between voting and their own lives, they will respond.

We have learned that we can take volunteers who are registering voters at a site, bring them in for an hour of training in which we teach them some simple but effective techniques, and send them back out to register three times as many people per hour.

Myth #2: Even if you register poor people, they still won't vote.

When Project VOTE! was getting off the ground, I can't tell you how many times we heard people say, "Maybe you can register people on food stamp lines, but they'll never vote." And our first test seemed to indicate these people were right. In 1981 we registered 2,000 voters in a special Congressional election in Prince Georges County, Maryland; with no follow-up, 82 percent stayed home.

We wanted to know if we were making voters or just making work for the Boards of Elections. So we did another test in New Jersey during the 1981 gubernatorial race. We divided our registrants into test groups and then sampled election records to see how many people in each test group had actually voted.

With only a letter from Coretta King, we had a 29 percent

198

turnout. With a couple of phone calls we were able to raise that number to 66 percent—in a state election with no federal race on the ballot.

In a similar test in 1984, we learned two interesting things: (1) that even without follow-up, our registrants will turn out at much higher rates—65 to 70 percent—in a presidential election than in a state or local race; and (2) that with follow-up voter education, we were able to achieve turnouts of 82 to 87 percent, and this among a group whose turnout would have been zero because they were not even registered when we found them.[6]

Project VOTE! puts an enormous amount of energy into follow-up voter education. We computerize the name, address, and phone number of everyone we register, along with information about the kinds of site at which we registered them, whether in a food stamp line, an unemployment line, a door-to-door registration drive, or a minority church. New registrants receive three rounds of nonpartisan voter education phone calls. Because we know where they were registered, we can begin the conversation at the point where our registration conversation left off—with issues we know they care about, issues that affect their lives. And then we go back and sample election records to see who voted, so that we continually test and refine our follow-up education strategies.

Myth #3: By its nature, voter registration by volunteers is a decentralized activity that cannot be tightly measured, monitored, or controlled.

On the contrary, voter registration can and must be a tightly managed enterprise.

Project VOTE! typically begins by pulling together a local coalition of groups committed to registering low-income and minority voters and working with the local coalition to agree on a coherent plan and goals—goals that force everyone to "stretch" beyond what is "known to be possible." Then we establish week-by-week, site-by-site objectives that permit continual monitoring.

The daily calls and frequent on-site visits from our field director to our regional directors and from our regional directors to our local staff become a key vehicle for monitoring progress and fixing problems. Equally important, they enable us to go beyond training workshops to provide the ongoing supervision that is so critical to effective on-the-job training.

Because all our registration is computerized, we know that the numbers being reported by our coordinators are real. But our monitoring doesn't stop with registration numbers. Each week we know how many volunteers have been recruited and how many volunteer hours have been contributed in each locality. And we know how many registrations have been produced per volunteer hour at each food stamp line or unemployment office or other site. This kind of information allows us to pinpoint problems and to ask the questions needed to help find ways to constantly improve the performance of each local project.

It also changes what our volunteers and staff are doing even before the information reaches us. For example, we talked ourselves blue in the face trying to convince volunteers that they needed to be recruiting other volunteers while they were out registering voters. We got nowhere—until we placed an item for "number of volunteers recruited" on the form they fill out when they finish volunteering at a site. That little addition to the form did what we had been unable to do through other kinds of persuasion: It changed the volunteers' definition of their responsibilities so that recruiting new volunteers finally became a part of what it meant to be doing a good job as a volunteer.

Myth #4: People won't volunteer in minority communities anymore; they have to be paid to register voters.

When we go into a new area, we will usually be told that we are going to have to pay people either a bounty per registration or an hourly wage if we want them to register voters. And, in many communities, there is, in fact, a tradition that, in races where the political establishment wants to see high voter turnout, bounties are paid. The trouble with paying for voter registration work is that in the long run it is disempowering to the community; it builds no pool of volunteers who will be available when no one from outside is offering a bounty. This actually makes it harder to find volunteers in the future.

Project VOTE! pays local organizers to recruit, train, and supervise volunteers. But all of the actual voter contact work is done by volunteers.

We have learned that one of the most important contributions we can make is to help local groups go beyond their traditional core of activists and their existing levels of skill in recruiting volunteers and increasing voter participation.

In many communities, lists of past activists suffer from the same problem as direct-mail lists: Once you get on them, you get called again and again and again. If you are not on the list, you are unlikely to be asked to help. We find we can greatly expand the pool of activists, for example, by helping organizations learn to effectively phone bank their entire membership list instead of just calling those who've been active before, and by teaching them to ask everyone they come into contact with—whether at a bus stop or while registering voters—to volunteer.

We've even learned that we can recruit about 10 percent of the people we call from cold lists of all registered voters in low-income and minority areas. The volunteers recruited in these voter registration efforts become an important community resource, to be called upon for future efforts.

Myth #5: Voter participation work ends on election day.

If we are sincere in our commitment to empowerment, we must continue to work with local groups after the election to help them make the transition between voter participation work and advocacy. We tell each new voter that his or her vote will make a difference; then we must help that voter follow through with elected officials to make sure it really does. When we go back to these same voters in the next election, we had better have something to show for the votes they cast the last time around.

This accountability of elected officials is, to some extent, already on the agenda of the local groups who form Project VOTE! coalitions. Yet these efforts are sporadic and uncoordinated. The close working relationship during the voter registration campaign tends to fall apart between elections.

In Illinois, to address this ongoing problem we intend to launch the Illinois Black Non-Partisan Political Network to sustain communication among communities between elections. It will be structured as a network so as to enhance rather than threaten the autonomy of participating groups, thereby permitting them to address the concerns of their members.[7]

Together we should be able to hold elected officials' feet to the fire more effectively than we could do it individually. Moreover, we need to make sure that voting by poor and minority communities results in tangible changes.

What the Future Holds

I mentioned earlier that the number of voters that we at Project VOTE! and the National Coalition and Southwest Voter and other organizations can register in 1988 could make a tremendous difference—that in each of the non-incumbent presidential elections since 1952, a shift of 87,000 votes or less would have changed the outcome. At Project VOTE!, our role is not to help any candidate or party but to prevent the tragic distortion of the democratic process that occurs when low-income and minority voters are stuck outside the political process.

In 1984 Project VOTE! coalitions registered 528,951 voters in three months. This year, 1988, we are already up and rolling, and we intend to beat that record. We'll be working in New Jersey, Pennsylvania, Illinois, Texas, Mississippi, Rhode Island, Tennessee, Washington, Michigan, Georgia, and possibly in

Florida, Nebraska, North Carolina, Louisiana, and Delaware, and in other states as well.[8] In a number of these states, the voters we register may hold the balance of power in Senate and House races, as well as in the presidential election.[9]

I want to urge each and every one of you to get involved, whether through Project VOTE! or another registration group working in your area. People who don't know where their next meal is coming from are counting on us to help them make democracy work.

Let us not step back from it. The future is at stake.

Notes

1. During 1984, local Project VOTE! coalitions that helped register more than a half-million voters were operating in Wilmington, Delaware; Gary, Indiana; Providence, Rhode Island; Portland and Augusta, Maine; Detroit, Michigan; Trenton, New Jersey; and cities throughout California, Illinois, Iowa, Maryland, Missouri, New Hampshire, Ohio, Pennsylvania, Tennessee, Texas, and Virginia.

2. The facts and statistics cited in this sentence and in subsequent bullet items were derived from in-house Project VOTE! analyses.

3. As of March 1992, the number of low-income and minority voters that Project VOTE! brought into the political process (however they may have chosen to vote) has exceeded the winning margin in four Senate races, five House races, more than 40 state and local elections, and one gubernatorial race.

4. Sandy Newman established Project VOTE! in 1981. The organization is headquartered in Washington, D.C.

5. As of March 1992, Project VOTE! has registered more than 1.4 million new low-income and minority voters. The organization's follow-up voter education program, according to actual samplings of election records, has produced turnouts of 85 percent.

6. These 1981 and 1984 test results are discussed in an in-house paper entitled, "Project VOTE! Voter Turnout Studies: A Summary."

7. As a result of the author's death, this project was never implemented.

8. Because of inadequate funding, Project VOTE! was forced to scale back registration drives in 1988. Nevertheless, the organization did register more than 364,000 voters in all the states mentioned except Delaware.

9. Project VOTE! voters did hold the balance of power in one Congressional race in 1988, that of Representative Peter Hoagland in the 2nd District of Nebraska.

Afterword

This book about the history of voting in the United States has been a story of effort and frustration, of defeat and triumph.

In February 1965, as a federal civil rights official, I helped conduct a hearing in Jackson, Mississippi, at which black citizens throughout the state testified about their efforts to register and vote. With quiet dignity and in words that were both matter-of-fact and eloquent, they told about being rebuffed, about the dangers they faced, and about why they kept coming back.

One witness, Unita Zelma Blackwell of Mayersville, Mississippi, gave an account of her repeated efforts, ultimately successful, to register herself and to encourage others to try as well. She spoke of the registrar requiring her to interpret technical provisions of the Mississippi constitution, of the fears of black citizens of Issaquena County that registration efforts would mean a cut-off of welfare checks in the winter when farm work was not available, of white men flashing shotguns and making threats. And yet she and others persisted because:

> "It is very important to have the people represented, and I wants somebody to represent me."

As to the threats:

> "You just get to the place you know it's going to happen, but you've just got to stand up and got to do something."

Twenty-seven years later, in June 1992, the MacArthur Foundation announced the award of one of its 33 "genius grants" to Unita Blackwell, who had become the first black woman elected mayor in Mississippi. The announcement stated:

> She succeeded in having her town [Mayersville] incorporated, making it eligible for federal funds and

205

then raised money to provide for basic services such as water, sewage and housing. She continues to work at the local level to create an economic and social infrastructure, while providing a national leadership example.

And yet in 1992 the shining "leadership example" of Unita Blackwell and others like her is unknown to hundreds of thousands of her fellow citizens who do not vote. For these citizens, in Harlem and the barrios of San Antonio and in South Central Los Angeles, the barriers to voting are not the perils of physical harassment or economic reprisal. Rather, these citizens are disfranchised by racial isolation, by a sense that the political system will not and perhaps cannot address their fundamental needs and by a disconnectedness from the civic life of the nation. Nor is their alienation ungrounded in the current political reality—a reality marked by the pervasive influence of money in the electoral process, the absence of institutional and political leadership at the local and national levels that voices the concerns of the poor, and the cynical use of racial polarization as a tool for political advantage. All of these factors make it difficult to argue persuasively to those worse off in society that their participation will be rewarded by responsiveness to their needs and concerns.

The dangers of nonparticipation, of a sense of ruthlessness that extends beyond minorities and poor people to the young and others in the nation, should not be underestimated. In this volume, Bill Clinton speaks of the need to "preserve the idea of the United States of America." In a global economy where wealth and those who possess it move easily across national boundaries, democratic participation is one of the few unifying principles that supports the "idea of the United States of America." As participation is weakened, the idea is weakened as well.

But even in difficult times, the struggle continues. In 1992 the Congress is busy renewing and extending provisions of the Voting Rights Act that make the ballot accessible to Native Americans, Hispanic Americans, Asian Americans, and Alaskan Natives. In addition, for the first time ever, Congress passed a statute mandating registration by mail and at government offices, provisions that would have facilitated participation by low-income, minority, and disabled citizens. A veto by President Bush simply means that the effort will continue. And efforts are also under way to repair the damage done by recent Supreme Court decisions that allow gains in the election of minorities to be diluted by stripping officeholders of some of their authority.

It is this theme of constant struggle that provides the continuity in the story of voting participation from Revolutionary times to the Civil War, from the campaign for women's suffrage to the battles against the white primary, the poll tax, and the literacy test. As long as there are those willing to continue the struggle, the idea of a democratic nation retains vitality and is renewed.

William L. Taylor
Vice President
Leadership Conference Education Fund

About the Contributors

Arnold Aronson is president of the Leadership Conference Education Fund, and the originator of the Bicentennial Conference. In 1950, Aronson, who was with the National Jewish Community Relations Council, together with A. Philip Randolph of the Brotherhood of Sleeping Car Porters, AFL, and Roy Wilkins of the NAACP, founded the Leadership Conference on Civil Rights, the largest, oldest, and most broadly based coalition in the country seeking to achieve "equality in a free, plural, democratic society." Aronson served as Secretary of LCCR until his retirement in 1982 and since then has served on LCCR's Executive Committee as honorary chairperson. He was a founder and member of the Executive Committee of the National Urban Coalition, a founder and member of the Board of the National Committee Against Discrimination in Housing, and a founder and past President of the National Association of Human Rights Workers. Aronson played a key role in the organization of the 1963 March on Washington.

Karen McGill Arrington is deputy director of the Leadership Conference Education Fund and policy/research associate for the Leadership Conference on Civil Rights. She is author of the *Civil Rights Monitor*, a newsletter about the civil rights activities of the federal government. Ms. Arrington served as the education monitor for the U.S. Commission on Civil Rights prior to its reconstitution in 1983.

Mary Frances Berry is the Geraldine R. Segal Professor of American Social Thought and professor of history at the University of Pennsylvania. Since 1980, she has served as a commissioner on the U.S. Commission on Civil Rights. In 1983, when President Ronald Reagan fired her and other commissioners who were outspoken critics of the administration's civil rights policies, she was reinstated by a federal district court. Congress later

208

reappointed her to the reconstituted commission. Dr. Berry is also one of the founders of the Free South Africa movement.

Bill Clinton is (as of this writing) the 42nd governor of Arkansas and the Democratic nominee for the presidency in 1992. He is only the second person in the state's history to be elected to four terms as governor, and the first to serve a four-year term in this century. A Rhodes scholar at Oxford University, he earned his bachelor's degree from Georgetown University and his law degree from Yale University. In 1976 he was elected attorney general and won his first term as governor in 1978 at the age of 32.

Henry Der is the executive director of Chinese for Affirmative Action (CAA), a San Francisco-based civil rights organization dedicated to promoting equal opportunities for Asian Americans in employment, education, voting rights, mass media reform, and access to social services. He has held this position since 1977. Mr. Der served as a Peace Corps volunteer in Kenya from 1968 to 1970, taught English as a second language to Chinese adult immigrants in vocational training programs, and joined CAA in 1973 as project director of its Right to Read Project.

Armand Derfner is an attorney in private practice in South Carolina. He specializes in civil rights, especially voting rights litigation. He has argued five voting rights cases before the Supreme Court, has written and lectured about voting rights, and was directly involved in the efforts to extend and amend the Voting Rights Act in 1982. Mr. Derfner has worked for several civil rights organizations, including the Lawyers Constitutional Defense Committee of the ACLU, the Lawyers Committee for Civil Rights Under Law, and the Joint Center for Political and Economic Studies.

209

Margaret Edds is a journalist who writes for the *Virginian-Pilot/ Ledger-Star*. She is the author of *Free At Last: What Really Happened When Civil Rights Came to Southern Politics*. Writing under a grant from the Alicia Patterson Foundation, Ms. Edds spent a year traveling throughout the seven states originally covered in the Voting Rights Act—Virginia, Georgia, North and South Carolina, Mississippi, Alabama, and Louisiana.

Lani Guinier is an assistant professor of law at the University of Pennsylvania Law School. From 1981 to 1988 she was assistant counsel for the NAACP Legal Defense and Educational Fund, Inc. She managed the voting rights docket for that organization and litigated primarily in the voting rights area. Major reported cases include *Thornburg* v. *Gingles*, *Harris* v. *Graddick*, and *Major* v. *Treen*. Ms. Guinier served as special assistant to the assistant attorney general for civil rights at the U.S. Department of Justice from 1977 to 1981.

Charles V. Hamilton is the Wallace S. Sayre Professor of Government at Columbia University. He is the author of six books, including *Adam Clayton Powell, Jr.: The Political Biography of an American Dilemma*; *The Bench and the Ballot: Southern Federal Judges and Black Voters*; and *The Black Experience in American Politics*. He received his Ph.D. from the University of Chicago and has taught at several universities, including Tuskegee, Rutgers, Lincoln (Pennsylvania), and Roosevelt, his undergraduate alma mater.

Judge Damon Keith has served on the U.S. Court of Appeals for the Sixth Circuit since his appointment by President Jimmy Carter in 1977. He was named to the U.S. District Court, Eastern District of Michigan, by President Lyndon Johnson in 1967. He was also chairman of the Judicial Conference on the Bicentennial of the United States Constitution. Judge Keith has published numerous articles on the law, racism, and civil rights, including "What Happens to a Dream Deferred: An Assessment of Civil Rights Law Twenty Years After the 1963 March on Washington" (*Harvard Civil Rights/Civil Liberties Law Review*, Vol. 19, No. 2, Summer 1984).

David Kusnet is a political consultant and speechwriter, currently serving as a speechwriter for Bill Clinton. He is the author of *Speaking American: How the Democrats Can Win in the Nineties*, as well as numerous articles that have appeared in *The Washington Post*, *The Baltimore Sun*, and *The New Republic*. Mr. Kusnet was a speechwriter for Democratic presidential candidates Walter Mondale and Michael Dukakis, and he served as vice president for communications for People for the American Way.

Celinda Lake is a partner and vice-president at Greenberg-Lake, The Analysis Group, Inc., a national Democratic polling firm based in Washington, D.C. Prior to joining that firm, Ms. Lake was political director at the Women's Campaign Fund; research director at the Institute for Social Research in Ann Arbor, Michigan; a policy analyst for the Subcommittee on Select Education; and chief analyst on the polling team at Peter Hart Research, Inc., for the Mondale/ Ferraro campaign.

Al Raby—one of the two men to whom this book is dedicated—was chairman of the board of directors of Project VOTE! during the last three years of his life. Project VOTE!'s primary goal is the registration of minorities and the poor so they will participate in the election process. He was also chairman of the Woodstock Institute, a private research organization concentrating on the economic impact of banking policies and investments, and was a partner in the private consulting firm of Coffey, Kay and Raby. Mr. Raby was the late Chicago mayor Harold Washington's 1983 campaign manager and served as the director of the Chicago Commission on Human Relations under Mayor Washington.

211

William L. Taylor is a lawyer, teacher, and writer in the fields of civil rights and education. He is vice president of the Leadership Conference Education Fund, a vice chair of the executive committee of the Leadership Conference on Civil Rights, and a member of the Citizens Commission on Civil Rights. He began his legal career in 1954 as an attorney on the staff of the NAACP Legal Defense and Educational Fund. In the 1960s he served as general counsel and later as staff director of the U.S. Commission on Civil Rights. In 1970 Mr. Taylor founded the Center for National Policy Review, a civil rights research and advocacy organization.

Eddie N. Williams has been president of the Joint Center for Political and Economic Studies since 1972. Located in Washington, D.C., the Joint Center is a national, nonprofit and nonpartisan research and public policy institution that conducts research and analyses on major policy issues that affect both black Americans and the nation as a whole. He is a founding member of the Black Leadership Forum, a coalition of the most influential national black public-service organizations in the United States. He is also chairman of the National Coalition on Black Voter Participation. Between 1968 and 1972, Williams was vice president for public affairs and director of the Center for Policy Study at the University of Chicago. In the 1960s, he held several positions in the U.S. Department of State and the U.S. Senate Committee on Foreign Relations.

Jeanette Wolfley is general counsel for the Shoshone-Bannock Tribes of the Fort Hall Indian Reservation located in southeastern Idaho. She is also an adjunct professor in the political science department at Idaho State University. Ms. Wolfley worked with the Native American Rights Fund from 1982 to 1988 as staff attorney and deputy director. She received her undergraduate degree from the University of Minnesota and her J.D. degree from the University of New Mexico Law School.

212

Other Leadership Conference Publications

Civil Rights Monitor, a newsletter on the federal government's civil rights activities

Civil Rights Perspectives, essays on civil rights and social justice issues

Joint Center Publications of Related Interest

FOCUS, a monthly magazine on politics and policy issues of concern to black Americans

Black Elected Officials: A National Roster, 1991

Elected and Appointed Black Judges in the United States, 1991, prepared in cooperation with The Judicial Council of the National Bar Association

Black State Legislators: A Survey and Analysis of Black Leadership in State Capitals, by David Bositis

"Keep Hope Alive!" —Super Tuesday and Jesse Jackson's 1988 Campaign for the Presidency, by Penn Kimball

Blacks and the 1992 Democratic National Convention

Blacks and the 1992 Republican National Convention

For more information about Leadership Conference publications, write the Leadership Conference Education Fund, 2027 Massachusetts Ave., N.W., Washington, D.C. 20036. For Joint Center publications, write the Joint Center for Political and Economic Studies, 1090 Vermont Ave., N.W., Suite 1100, Washington, D.C. 20005.